Real Magnolias

Other books by Becky Freeman

Worms in My Tea and Other Mixed Blessings

Adult Children of Fairly Functional Parents

Marriage 9-1-1

Still Lickin' the Spoon

A View from the Porch Swing

Courage for the Chicken-Hearted

Real Magnolias

Stories of Southern Women Finding Hope, Love, and Laughter

Becky Freeman

A
JANET
THOMA
BOOK

THOMAS NELSON PUBLISHERS
Nashville

Published in association with the literary agency of Alive Communications, 1465 Kelly Johnson Blvd., #320, Colorado Springs, CO 80920.

Library of Congress Cataloging–in–Publication Data

Freeman, Becky, 1959–
    Real magnolias: stories of Southern women finding hope, love, and laughter / Becky Freeman.
      p. cm.
    Includes bibliographical references (p.).
    ISBN 0-7852-7567-3 (PB)
    1. Women—Southern States—Biography. 2. Women—Southern States—Conduct of life. 3. Freeman, Becky, 1959– . I. Title.
HQ1438.S63F74 1999
305.4'0975—dc21

                    98–53421
                    CIP

For my sister, Rachel, the next writing Magnolia in our family tree. Words cannot express my love for you, and how proud I am to be your sister.

Contents

Part 3: Magnolias Floating from the Family Tree

Part 4: Georgia Girls' Reunion

Acknowledgments

Like a crazy quilt, each piece of this book was stitched together with the love, prayers, and input of a circle of family and friends.

To each featured Magnolia, my heartfelt gratitude for your courage in sharing these stories, and for your general enthusiasm and insightful suggestions.

A special thanks to my mother, Ruthie, and my sister, Rachel, who, along with Gracie Malone, Brenda Waggoner, and Melissa Gantt, pitched in emergency help with editing whenever I called and yelped, "9-1-1!"

Greg Johnson, my agent, has truly been heaven-sent. He's been amazing, kind, and patient while helping this scatter-brained author to focus.

Janet Thoma's consistent belief in me as a writer, and her unfailing support of this project, means more to me than words can express.

To my ever-lovin', ever-patient husband and kids: I know you'll be thrilled to have Mom back in the kitchen and out of her office. As a matter of fact, I'm going to go burn up a batch of homemade cookies just for you right this minute.

With love and grins,

Becky

What is it about Southern women?
—Becky Freeman

Fried Green Magnolias

What is it about Southern women?

From *Gone With the Wind* to *Steel Magnolias* to *Fried Green Tomatoes,* most women admit there's a definite mystique, a universal curiosity, about what goes on below the Mason-Dixon line—in that charming, antebellum world known as the South (be it the Old South, New South, Deep South, or Down South).

For three years I've written a monthly column, "Marriage 9-1-1," in a Southern-based publication (*Home Life* magazine, Nashville, TN), so most of my invitations to speak come from magnolia country. I love to go and share stories at churches and retreats or the ever-popular "Ladies' Night Out."

Though most of the events are variations on a standard theme—decorations, door prizes, music, food (usually salad, supper and dessert), laughter, and spiritual lessons—each gathering is unique, each woman a blessing. I can't imagine kinder, more loving and genuine hostesses and audiences. And funnnnnnnny—oh, my. Even without trying, humor has a way of ping-ponging between me and my newfound friends wherever I go.

At a recent banquet where I gave the keynote, a few men kindly offered to unload my suitcase of books for the table. Before long, the hostess came up to me laughing. "Becky," she said, "I told everybody to be ready for anything when you arrived. The deacons just unloaded a bra with your books."

I blushed, but then, relaxed. After all, I knew from experience I was among friends.

Later that evening I visited the church's craft sale corner, purchasing a cute wooden country-style Santa mounted on a ribbon-wrapped book. As I drove home, I glanced over at my purchase and then did a double take when I spied the title along the spine of the leather volume which the church ladies had used for the craft. In bright gold letters, above the gaily checked ribbon, it read *Gonococcal Urethritis in the Male.*

The night I accidentally left my lapel mike on while I was in the ladies room, is not one I—or the audience—is likely to forget. Thankfully, I was among sweet Southern Baptist women, who enjoy a good laugh as much as a good sermon, and they loved me in spite of knowing more about me than they ever wanted to know.

Wanting to be helpful, I brought a salad to a recent event to add to the buffet. Within minutes I heard the ladies laughing. "Becky!" they exclaimed. "Is this your salad?"

"Yes," I answered. "Why?"

"There's a big pair of silver earrings in it. We figured it had to be yours."

It is such experiences, unplanned and so human, that bond us together as sisters—with our feet firmly potted in clay.

I've discovered that behind the "froufrouiest" of hairdos, beneath the lace and flowered print dresses and broad-brimmed hats of Southern charm—lie women who love to laugh at themselves, with hearts that need and want to give love, and who ache when life hurts. Women who struggle with doubt and failure, even as they reach out in faith to an all-loving, all-forgiving God. In a word, these women are *real.*

This afternoon I enjoyed a delightful lunch with two ladies I'd never met before today, and within a few minutes—before I'd even mentioned I was writing this book—we were deep into a conversation about women of the South and movies that depict them. One of the young women, Carman, remarked with a delicate flick of her wrist, "My husband's so funny. The other night I told him I was going out to rent a 'woman movie' and he said, 'You gonna get *Fried Green Magnolias* or *Steel Green Tomatoes* this time?'"

I laughed as I realized these movies probably spawned the term "chick flicks." Men not only have a hard time pronouncing the titles, they are perplexed at our love for what most guys see as mushy, sappy, weep-a-thons.

But any woman who's had her hair done in a small town beauty shop (be it in Wisconsin or Georgia) can relate to the soap opera drama of the beauty shop scenes in *Steel Magnolias*—where Dolly Parton wielded her brush and hairspray as well as she handed out sage advice.

Is there a woman alive—above or below the Mason-Dixon line—who didn't sob through two hankies as the grieving mother, poignantly played by Sally Field, screamed and flailed as she fully mourned the loss of her grown daughter within the love, acceptance, tears—and yes, even the laughter—of her closest circle of friends? (I'm beginning to realize laughter and tears make up the raindrops that water the friendships of women.)

For anyone who's ever been lost in midlife, Jessica Tandy's maternal friendship to Kathy Bates in the nursing home scenes from *Fried Green Tomatoes,* touched a poignant longing we never outgrow—the need for a mentoring, navigating soul.

For women struggling to find courage to pick up life's pieces, there's Scarlett O'Hara. With flaws bigger than her hooped skirts she still managed to inspire us for more than five decades, to rise from the ashes with renewed hope, for "Tomorrow," after all, "is another day."

Southern scenes, Southern stories, Southern women—universal application. In a similar way, it is my hope that this written collection will open the curtain on Southern scenes, interesting stories and special ladies—whose friendships are quilted together by threads of love and faith. And that these stories will touch the hearts of women from California to Virginia, from sea to shining sea and beyond with their universal application.

I've loved the process of writing this book, beyond any writing experience I've had before. Writing can be a solitary profession, but not so this time around. I often had the sense company was near as I wrote—feeling emotionally and prayerfully embraced by those whose stories I am privileged to share.

Like a gathering of women in a small town beauty shop, each friend and family member presented in these pages has their own fascinating story to tell, and some of their stories even intertwine.

All have qualities of vulnerability, humor, and life-worn faith.

Each of them, in some special way, has been a Real Magnolia to me.

I've divided these chapters into four sections. First, you'll meet the Georgia Girls, a group of friends who served as the initial inspiration for this book.

The next section introduces friends and role models who have affected my life in a deep way, calling me toward growth and authenticity, or expanding my capacity to love.

So much of who I am and what I do comes from the wild and wonderful women in my family tree. How privileged I am to share their stories with you in Part Three.

Finally, you won't want to miss the last two chapters or the surprises that await when the Georgia Girls meet, one year later, for a very special reunion.

Just for fun, I've added a page or two, at the end of each chapter, of quotes, poems, or letters that emphasize the main thought from each woman's story.

So come on in to this beauty parlor of a book. Join in the wit and wisdom you can only get in the company of a bunch of fun female friends. If your experience *reading* these stories is anything like mine has been *writing* them, you'll laugh and you'll cry—and you will leave feeling utterly gorgeous, inside and out.

And then, I hope, you'll call a girlfriend and plan a special day together. To stop and smell the roses, or better yet, *shop* and smell the magnolias.

Observations on Southern Charm

As you may have noticed with some dismay, most Southerners would rather be charming than rich. They believe that you can devote your energies to making money or to being delightful, but you can't really do both.

I had forgotten how pervasive and powerful this lifestyle is until I moved back to my hometown—Savannah—after several uneasy years in the North. In the languorous old seaport, the output of charm *per capita* is unbelievable. Visitors are often struck by such a deluge of it that they go bobbing around, dazed and helpless, like bewildered cherries in a sea of whipped cream. When there are no visitors, Savannians keep in practice by charming one another.

At first, exposure to such expert charmers can be delightful. You feel flattered, uplifted, bemused, and enchanted. You never dreamed that you were so good-looking, so witty, so irresistible. It takes a while for the dark realization to creep in that, as a matter of fact, you're not . . .

(But) charm isn't all playacting or self-centeredness. Charm is also a reaching out. It's a small voice saying, "Look, I'm aware of you. I know you're there. I want you to like me, sure—but I also want you to feel easier about yourself."

Call it charm, call it caring, it's something we need badly in this mechanized, fragmented, dehumanized world.[1]

—*Arthur Gordon*

Part 1

The Georgia
Girls' Getaway

Isn't life such a blessin'?
—Maureen York

Maureen and a satisfied little customer, John Byron.

Blessin's in Bloom

*T*he answering machine light was blinking. I love it when that happens. It's like coming home to a fire in the hearth or food on the table or a letter in the mailbox. (There's something lonely about coming home to an empty phone recorder; feels a bit like rejection, like nobody wants you.) I sat down on the side of the bed and pressed *Play*.

"Hello, Becky," the voice rang with a familiar drawl. "Are you ready for a blast from the past? This is Suzanne Forster!"

Suzanne and I had been good friends during the brief time we both lived near the little West Texas town of Boyd. Her husband, Garth, pastored our small congregation at Pleasant Grove Baptist Church Number Two. (Which backed up, as most little country churches do, to a cemetery bearing an equally charming name. We never figured out what happened to Pleasant Grove Baptist Church Number One, however. Maybe it died and became the cemetery.)

Though young in the ministry, Garth was a natural, insightful teacher. He and Suzanne, ever kind and generous and just plain fun, soon became one of our favorite couples.

Scott and I were in the thick of our own private baby boom

when we lived near the Forsters. I was either chasing a preschooler, potty training a toddler, nursing an infant, or incubating new life. Suzanne and Garth were great with our kids, longing for the day when they would have a child of their own. I could not imagine two people more suited to parenting, but as time passed, it looked as though this might not be in God's plan. *Infertility. Childlessness.* These are heart-wrenching words for couples aching to start a family. I prayed over and over that God would bless our friends with a house full of kids.

Within two years of our first meeting, Garth and Suzanne moved back home to Alabama where their folks lived, eventually landing a pastorate in the magnolia-lined, Mayberry-like community of Barnesville, Georgia. Scott and I stayed in Texas, but headed to the eastern part of the state. Somehow, with the moves and other changes in our lives, we lost track of each other for nearly a decade.

Of all places, the Forsters found me again in *Worms in My Tea*—surprised to discover I'd moved on from actually burping and diapering and chasing babies to writing about these experiences in humorous detail.

I dialed the number Suzanne left, and within a few minutes we were visiting as though we'd seen each other only yesterday.

Suzanne asked about Scott's work and our kids, and then I had to ask the question I dreaded. "And do you have children?"

"Well," Suzanne said, "as a matter of fact we do. A son, Brent, who is seventeen now and a daughter, Savannah, who is six."

I mentally calculated the years since we'd seen each other and something didn't add up.

"But how could you possibly have a teenager?"

"There's kind of an amazing story behind that."

"I happen to love amazing stories," I said, my interest piqued.

"Then I have a proposition for you. Come to Georgia and I'll fill in the details of our kids over a glass of sweet tea. There's more to it than I can share on the phone."

"Actually," I thought aloud, "I have to be in Atlanta for a book convention in a few weeks. My sister Rachel was going to meet me there—flying down from Virginia—and we thought we'd have a girls' getaway."

"Then have I got the place for you," Suzanne said, as she unplugged all the stops and poured on the sales pitch. "Listen to this. Callaway Gardens in Pine Mountain, Georgia, is a short scenic drive from Atlanta. There are luxury condos nestled among the trees; flower, herb and vegetable gardens; a butterfly sanctuary; a chapel on the lake; shopping; restaurants and . . ."

"Sold!" I interrupted, before she could finish the verbal tour.

"You won't be sorry," answered Suzanne. "You call Rachel, and I'm going to ask a few friends of mine to come too. We'll split the cost of the condo and have the time of our lives."

Two months later, Rachel and I found ourselves in Barnesville, Georgia, sitting in Suzanne's car, parked in front of a tan and white storybook cottage. I half-expected the gingerbread man to come running out the door.

As the driver and designated door knocker, Suzanne stepped out of the driver's seat and scooted up the porch to fetch her friend, Maureen. Maureen was not only Suzanne's neighbor and confidante, she was her hairdresser, or as Maureen preferred to be called, her "glamour technician." Rachel and I silently hoped Suzanne had good taste in choosing the other gals who would be sharing the Callaway condo.

When Maureen opened the front door, she didn't just walk down the steps—she *sashayed* down them on clouds of giggles. Rachel leaned over from her place in the front seat, gave me a knowing wink, and whispered, "She looks like *our* kind of gal." I nodded in eager agreement.

Maureen's hair was a perfectly coiffed ball of blond fluff. Scarlet lipstick outlined a smile as welcoming as a Southern summer morning. Her bountiful figure epitomized the word *voluptuous*. She smelled of honeysuckle and apple blossoms. If there had been a theme song to accompany Maureen's stroll down the sidewalk runway and into our lives, I'm sure it would have been, "I Enjoy Being a Girl."

The first words out of her bright red lips completed the charming picture. "Don't y'all just know this trip is going to be such a blessin'?"

Since our car was already bulging at the seams, Maureen and Susan, a Delta flight attendant, decided to take their own vehicle. We'd have to get acquainted with Susan later, as we needed to get on the road before dark. Tina, the last of the Georgia Girls, would meet us later for supper.

Suzanne followed close behind Maureen and Susan's vehicle. As we drove among emerald hills and through quaint little towns, we watched in amazement the drama playing out in the car in front of us. Red fingernails flying, blond hair just a-bobbing, two mouths that never closed. Astounding, how Southern women can talk, listen, let the paint on their nails dry, and drive a vehicle all at the same time.

I glanced around inside our car full of women. All of us were visibly straining towards the car in front of us, as though, if we leaned forward enough, we could somehow catch the good pieces of gossip flying between Maureen and Susan.

Exhausted from a long week at the convention, I fell asleep in the backseat. I came to consciousness only after I felt the car come to a complete stop, and heard the excitement of four newly released women—sprung, as it were, from their black-and-white routines into a vacation of living color.

First stop: quaint bookstore.

"To see if they have your books, Hon," Maureen said, poking her head through the backseat window. I gave her a sleepy, questioning look.

While they chatted among themselves, I scrounged for my

makeup bag to no avail. Finally giving up, I tagged behind the waddling, cackling gaggle of women. As soon as we hit the bookstore, we dispersed—me to look for a mirror, the others to check out the book stock.

"Excuse me," said Maureen, flashing her brilliant smile at the unsuspecting clerk, "but do you have any books by Becky Freeman? Because you see, she's OUR friend and a WON-duhful writer."

"Hmmm, I may have one," said the clerk nonchalantly. "Look ovuh they-uh on that rack."

Sure enough. There I was. In living print. *Now can we go?* I wanted to ask. *Why is it I'm always caught without makeup and dressed in an old sweatshirt whenever I'm called upon to act famous?*

Too late. The clerk held a copy of *Marriage 9-1-1* in her hand, flipped it over, and examined the photo on the back. My *glamour* photo. She looked at me, in all my disheveled reality, then back at the book and declared, "This picture don't look nothin' like you."

I don't know why I didn't just say, "You're right. It isn't. We were just playing a little joke on you," and be done with it. But I have this deeply bred Southern trait: I want people to like me, to believe me, and—if at all possible—to love and cherish me. If I were a homeless person, I'm convinced my hand lettered cardboard sign would read: "Will Work for Approval."

"Somebody hand me some lipstick quick," I whispered in desperation. Rachel obliged. I slid the color over my lips while Maureen worked on poufing my hair with her long fingernails. Then Susan, Suzanne, and Rachel took turns holding the book with my picture on it beside my authentic face.

"See!" I said in my most convincing voice. "It's really me. I'm the one who wrote this book. Really. I was just sleeping in the car and my face is a little tired so I don't look quite as perky as I normally look."

"Actually," said my sister, "there's this little upholstery pattern embedded on your right cheek that looks rather nice."

"Very funny," I shot back.

The clerk looked at the book once more then back at me and made her final judgment. "Don't look like you."

I couldn't believe it! All I could think of to say was, "Well, maybe I forgot who I am. I do forget things." Then I asked Rachel for fifty cents so I could go outside and buy myself a Mountain Dew. When in Rome—or in this case, the hills—do as the hillbillies do. The rest of the belles followed close behind in a protective huff.

"Well, I never!" said Maureen. "She was downright rude. Didn't know what she was talkin' about. What—was she BLIND? That picture looks just like you, Sweetie."

"I thought you perked up real nice once you put on the lipstick," added my sister thoughtfully.

"I smell barbecue," said Suzanne.

I was supremely grateful for the change of topic.

We walked over to a country-style roadside stand and ordered three barbecue sandwiches to split between the five of us—just a snack to tide us over until we got to Callaway.

As we sat around the picnic table in the warm late afternoon sun, Maureen let go with one of her famous laughs, looked at me and said, "Well, it's a blessin', darlin', that you have such a good sense of humor. Lots of women would be crying by now over that lady's insultin' remarks."

"Oh," I smiled back, wiping spicy red sauce from my chin. "It's all material. You watch, this episode will probably end up in a book somewhere, sometime."

Maureen offered a final consolation prize. She gave me her famous benediction once more, with feeling. "Honey, you're *such* a blessin'!"

Over the next few days together, we'd discover that most pleasant things—from a good laugh, to a soft rain, to high

cheekbones, to those "cute little specks of sage in the dressin'"—
were "blessin's" to Maureen.

There's an old hymn I sometimes hum to myself, "Showers
of Blessings." I used to sing the chorus as a child, though rather
absently, I must admit.

> *Showers of blessings,*
> *Showers of blessings we need.*
> *Mercy drops 'round us are falling,*
> *but for the showers we plead.[1]*

Then one day, I grasped the deeper meaning—the hymn-
writer was being sustained by "mercy drops," sprinkles of God's
goodness, but he was hungry for more. What he wanted to experience was a downpour of God Himself.

I went to that weekend exhausted and worn, hanging on to
the few "mercy drops" of spiritual water that had come my way
of late. But I was working up a powerful thirst in my inner soul.
Little did I know, just around these green mountains, inside a
land of butterflies and stately magnolias, some powerful cloud-
bursts were about to break over the horizon.

And with them, showers and showers of nonstop blessin's.

On Seeing Life's Blessin's

The love we give. The love given to us. Was it not a gift? And faith, that most primal of spiritual responses, did it not also come to us as a gift?

The air we breathe. A gift. The lungs to breathe it. A gift.

Our waking to a new day. A gift.

Whatever we start with, if we follow it far enough back, the source is God and His generosity in sharing it.

It's all a gift. Everything.

We live, quite literally, off His generous bounty.

So great the generosity. So little the gratitude. Yet still He gives.

Gift after gift after gift.[2]

—*Ken Gire*

"There are only two ways to live your life. One is as though nothing is a miracle. The other is as though everything is a miracle."[3]

—*Albert Einstein*

We began to pray for the impossible—
there was LOTS of impossible.
—Suzanne Forster

Suzanne, Brent, Becky, and Savannah

Sunflower Children

Now fully awake and aware, Rachel and I climbed back in the car. Suzanne Forster started the engine and headed the hood towards Pine Mountain.

"Okay, Suzanne," I said, peeking my head over the front seat.

"Okay, what?" she asked.

"Okay, I'm ready for the amazing story of your children."

"Well, it's pretty special. First, I wanted to tell you, though we never planned it this way, Maureen and Susan and I ended up being close friends in our small church—and all of us, for various reasons, could not have children. And so we began praying for each other even as we prayed for ourselves."

"Isn't it neat how God so often puts us with friends who understand us?"

"Oh, honey," she agreed. "I don't know what we'd have done without each other. We are literally praying children into each other's arms.

"Big Oak Ranch,[1] nestled in scenic Alabama, is run by an old high school friend of mine, John Croyle. John was a star college football player, with a heart as big as his talent. At one point, he put aside professional aspirations to fulfill another, stronger dream: to create a loving place for kids stuck in an awful 'no-kid's land'—without a safe place to belong. John's ranch for boys, and later, the ranch for girls, are two of the finest in the country.

"When I heard John speak on *The 700 Club*, I knew I had to call and see if there was anything I could do to help. He was thrilled, and hired me to be the educational coordinator for the school.

"And it was there at the ranch I met Brent: a nine-year-old, blue-eyed, towheaded kid, a soft-spoken little fellow with a heart of gold. I couldn't help feeling less like his teacher and more like his mother."

"Uh-oh," I said, stretching my legs on the car seat.

Suzanne laughed. "Yep. I knew Brent was what they call 'unadoptable'—both his parents were alive. In spite of my logic, I couldn't help my feelings.

"As it turned out, Brent had praying grandmothers who loved him dearly but were unable to care for him. His own parents, though middle class, were caught in such a web of addiction and dysfunction they realized Brent was better off somewhere stable—until such time as they got their own lives together. It's just that 'that time' never seemed to come.

"It was so hard to see such a kindhearted kid living outside of a regular family, especially when we had a nice home with two empty bedrooms and two open hearts."

Suzanne sighed before continuing. "Anyway, Garth and I began taking Brent on outings, having him over for the weekends. Then one night, as we were driving him back to the ranch, Brent turned those blue eyes up to mine and Garth's and asked, 'Do you think a guy like me could ever be adopted by somebody like you?'"

"Oh, Suzanne," Rachel and I both said with compassion.

"I know," Suzanne answered. "It broke our hearts. After we dropped Brent off, Garth and I agreed we had to do something.

"Soon after, I went to John's office and poured out my heart about Brent. 'Ah, that kid's an eagle,' I remember John saying, flashing that famous smile of his. 'Brent's destined to soar.'"

"And so?" Rachel asked.

"And so, day after day, I taught at the boys' ranch, and day after day, Brent stole another piece of my heart. We began to pray for the impossible—and there was LOTS of impossible. At one point, I said, 'Lord, maybe we've got our wires crossed. Brent has *living* parents. Do you see how crazy it is for me to try to adopt a boy with two parents and two grandparents? I am so tired of beating my head against closed doors.'

"I literally lay prostrate, asking God for some shred of encouragement. I opened my Bible to a passage I'd marked in Luke 21:14, 15. 'Therefore settle it in your hearts not to meditate beforehand on what you will answer; for I will give you a mouth and wisdom which all your adversaries will not be able to contradict or resist.'

"Within hours a call came in from Brent's paternal grandmother saying God had convinced her we were to be Brent's parents. His mother, Sandy, as well, was softening to the idea of allowing the adoption for the sake of her son, whom she loved but could not care for."

"Wow," I said. Rachel's echoed "Wow" was a heartbeat behind mine.

"By age twelve Brent was able to come live with us," continued Suzanne. "During that time we met Brent's mother, and though it was hard for her to give up parental rights to her son, she could see Brent was flourishing. Sandy's mother, Brent's grandmother, also knew we were the answer to her prayers for her grandson.

"I'll never forget sitting beside Brent as he told his biological mother, 'I love you, but Garth and Suzanne are my parents. I want a real home, Mom.' With tears streaming down her face, Brent's mother signed the papers and later, convinced his dad to do the same. It was truly an act of love on Sandy's part. Brent still corresponds with her and now both families are close.

"At age fourteen, Brent became fully, legally ours. But I knew, the moment I saw Brent, he was the son of my heart."

"I can't wait to meet him," I said. "He looks so handsome in the pictures you mailed me."

It was affirming to hear that, sometimes, even on this side of the rainbow, dreams really do come true.

"Now what about Savannah? Her picture is adorable." I showed Rachel the picture Suzanne had sent. She looked like a sunflower child. Big blue eyes, long blond curls, dimples big enough to fall into.

"Savannah came to us through a friend who rescued her from a horribly neglectful home. Brent quickly became her idol and friend. She is smart as a whip and sweet as sugar. But with all the issues of abandonment, Savannah also came with her share of vinegar.

"Still Garth and I loved her as our little girl, sharing hugs and kisses, and trying to hold steady through some showstopping poutings. She's quite the theatrical child.

"Then a few months after Savannah came to live with us, but before the adoption was final, I went to the doctor with some odd symptoms. I nearly fell over when she said, 'Suzanne, you are pregnant.'

"'I can't be pregnant!' I told her. 'We've been trying to conceive for seventeen years. I've never been pregnant before!'

"'Well, sometimes,' she said, 'the impossible happens.' Garth and I were beside ourselves with joy."

"I know you must have been," I said gently knowing, obviously, this baby's story did not have a fairy-tale ending.

Suzanne wiped away a tear. "I wanted that baby so very much. The emotional pain of high, high hopes and then . . ."

"I'm so sorry." I touched Suzanne's shoulder in a gesture of comfort. To say good-bye to the unborn child of your womb, and at the same time, welcome an adopted child of your heart, is about as emotional a seesaw as I could imagine.

Suzanne shook her head slowly, tapping the steering wheel thoughtfully. "I remember being hooked up to some machines at the hospital after we lost the baby, telling Garth he needed to call Brent at school before word in this small town reached him that I was in the hospital. When the principal called him to the office and I explained what happened over the phone, he cried.

"Becky, Brent cried for my loss. He felt my hurt. I wanted to leap through the phone and hold my son and never let go."

"Sometimes," I said, "our kids can be our angels of mercy. Their hearts are so tender . . ."

Suzanne reached in her purse and pulled out a well-worn piece of paper.

"I wrote these thoughts down late one night, a night when Savannah—in her own sweet way—also reached out to comfort me."

Tonight, at church, the focus of Garth's message was "The Sanctity of Human Life." As the service began, my six-year-old daughter was snuggled close beside me. As most young children tend to do, she had her hymnbook in her lap—a "desk" for the artwork she would quietly draw as her daddy preached.

In the first minutes of the service a friend stood to sing a moving song about a little one who will never be born because of abortion.

My thoughts drifted back to the previous spring. It was our first pregnancy in almost seventeen years of marriage. I was in awe as I saw the heart beating on the monitor at the doctor's office. Imagine, the blood that pumped through that tiny heart also pumped through my heart! After three months of loving care in my womb, the Lord took that little life home to be with Him.

The song ended and I looked at Savannah, my little girl, through tear-filled eyes.

She kissed my hand and smiled at me with a 'knowing' beyond her years. I pulled her close and whispered, "I'm so glad you're my baby!" She nestled more securely in my embrace as the Lord brought comfort to both of us in that moment.

On the way home I asked Savannah if she understood the words of the song—that they were from the perspective of a baby who would never be born because a mom chose not to let it live. She said, "Yes, Mommy, and it made us think of our baby in heaven with Jesus."

"Savannah," I said, "I love you more than you'll ever know. Your daddy and I are so very, very thankful your biological mother gave birth so you could be our very special daughter for life. Always remember, Sweetheart, it is not how you came into this world that makes you our daughter. God placed you in our family through a bond that He put in our hearts."

Even as I reminded my little girl tonight of her special place in our hearts, God reminded me of a very special lesson as well. At 39 years of age, I don't know that I will ever experience another life in my womb the way I did for a few precious weeks last spring. But the Lord is showing me over and over, that the organ of primary importance in the birth of a child is not the womb, but the heart. For it is in the heart that the life bond forms, where commitments are made.

I am twice blessed in this journey of life, with a precious son, and a beloved daughter—both born of my heart.

"That's absolutely beautiful," I said, quietly slipping the love-worn paper back to Suzanne.

I leaned back on the car seat and looked out the window.

The sun was setting behind a blue-green meadow, casting a celestial glow to the world. Silently, I thanked the Lord for answering the prayer I sent up from Boyd, Texas, more than a decade ago. I do not pretend to understand God's ways, why He took Garth and Suzanne's baby to heaven so soon, why Brent and Savannah had to live through difficult years before finding their "real" Mom and Dad.

But this one thing I do know: God has blessed my friends with children to love, and who love them back.

Like my own "angel kid," Gabriel, would say—in his matter-of-fact Texas drawl—"If you love each other, well shoot, that's all that matters."

Indeed, Gabe, indeed.

Letters Between Suzanne and Brent,
Mother and Son

My Dearest Son,

You will never know what a very special blessing you are to this mother's heart! From the earliest days of our meeting, I somehow knew God would bring us together as mother and son.

When you were only ten, you began to stay with us on weekends. Your bright blue eyes and winsome smile would charm everyone. Behind that whistling, blond exterior lurked an energetic, mischievous, very normal boy. You were kind and friendly, compassionate and loving; always in tune to the feelings of others, forgiving of anyone who has wronged you. It was obvious God's hand was on your life at an early age.

It's ironic that I am writing to you tonight, on what would have been your baby brother or sister's first birthday. As your dad and I told you when we were expecting, you will always be our firstborn—birthed in this family through the deep love that God placed in my heart for you. A son of tremendous promise!

No matter what the mood has been, we have started and ended every day as a family by exchanging "I love yous." I pray our home will always be a refreshing retreat for you in a sometimes crazy world.

Remember the following, that we framed for you on your adoption day?

Not flesh of my flesh, nor bone of my bone
but nevertheless God made you my own.
Never forget for a single minute,
you weren't born under my heart—but in it!
—*Anonymous*

Born from my heart, there to be a part—forever
and always—my one and only son!

Lovingly,
Mother
(October 1998)

Dear Mom and Dad,
Before I came to live with you, I was always moving from place to place. My biological mother loved me so much, but she couldn't provide a stable home. When I met you at Big Oak Ranch* and began spending time with you, I knew God had something bigger planned for my life. My first mother showed how much she loved me by allowing me to be adopted by you. You became my parents, helping me know I am your son. God has given us a deep sense of joy and love in this home.
I love you very much—thanks for loving me.

Your son,
Brent
(Age 17, October 1998)

*For more information on Big Oak Ranch, see Notes.

Sometimes I'm afraid I'll forget what he looked like—how it felt to rest my head on his chest.
—Tina Clark

Tina's favorite photo of Wyndell, her husband.

"I expect him to come out of it and just start talking to me."

Garden of Girlfriends

We drove into the entrance of Callaway Resort and stepped out into an enchanted forest. This beautiful retreat, nestled in the Georgia hills near President Roosevelt's favorite vacation spot, had obviously been built with love. (And a small family fortune.) A lovely chapel on the lake, made of hand-hewn timbers and imported stained glass, reflected the intention of the founders: to honor God, to allow others to stop and savor His beauty and goodness.

With a face of freshly applied makeup, a stout swig of Mountain Dew, lungs full of country air, an eyeful of blue mountain beauty, and an earful of chattering women—I was fast on my way to being a happy camper. Especially since our campsite would be a luxury cabin with carpeted living room, full-size kitchen, and two huge baths.

First stop: more food.

We met up with Tina at the Country Store & Kitchen. At first glance Tina seemed a little on the quiet side. Suzanne had told us she was a widow. Her husband Wyndell had died of a brain tumor in 1993, and she was left to raise their two boys, Logan and Seth, ages five and seven, on her own. I'd never met a widow my own age before, and I shot a private look at Rachel that said, in secret sister language, "Do you think she'll be fun?"

Little did we know. The waitress at the restaurant could not seat us all together, so Suzanne, Susan, and Maureen ate at one table, Tina and Rachel and I at another. Though her humor was dry and subtle, dark-eyed Tina had me and my sister chuckling through our appetizers of fried green tomatoes with rémoulade sauce; laughing through our main meal of chicken-fried steak, sweet potatoes, and turnip greens; and falling off our chairs by the time we dug into our apple dumplings with ice cream. I'm sure the other girls thought we'd been sipping muscadine wine, but all we were drinking was sweet peach tea.

While Tina Clark left to go powder her nose, Rachel and I privately concurred: The amount of *joie de vivre* in this brunette wonder was off the *carpe diem* charts.

My curiosity mounted as I went over the facts again. Tina was single, a full-time teacher to severely emotionally and mentally handicapped children. She was also a mother to two fatherless boys. She'd adored her handsome husband who was no longer around to lean upon. She had seen Wyndell through an ordeal that made the movie *My Life* look like a picnic in the park.

"If only Wyndell had died from a brain tumor as smoothly as that movie portrays," Tina had said. "It made everything seem too clean." The stories of the agony she and Wyndell went through would make a grown man weep. As horrendous as hearing about the physical pain was for me, the most heartbreaking was listening to Tina describe Wyndell's final good-byes to his young sons.

How does a father find the strength to say to his boys, "Son, I'm so sorry I will not be there to cheer at your first Little League game"? Or, "I love you so much and I am so, so sorry I won't be able to watch you grow up, to applaud at your graduation, or hug the girl you'll marry."

"A month after Wyndell died," Tina had shared, "our church

had an Easter egg hunt and in the midst of the festivities, I could not find Seth. Finally I found him, bless his heart, huddled up in a little ball, crying behind the church building. The sight of all those kids with daddies having a good time was just too over-whelming."

The loss for this young family was more than I could fathom. And so . . .

How was it that Tina Clark, *of all people*, possessed this larger-than-life capacity to enjoy the moment? More than any of us, she felt elation at the sight of an herb garden or the fragrance of a gardenia. I hoped to find out by the end of the weekend.

After dinner we drove to our condo under a night of velvet sky and crystal stars. The six of us pooled our camping know-how and built a fire in the living room fireplace. Well, actually, we turned on the gas logs, but we felt very Girl Scoutish all the same.

As Tina shared some of her students' antics, we laughed like a bunch of rowdy teenagers, comments flying fast and free. There in that living room we were suddenly completely safe to be exactly who we were. No need to measure our words, no one to sit in judgment. No one had to cook or clean or answer the phone or stop to settle an argument between kids. Just six gals in old T-shirts, painting our toenails and shootin' the breeze.

Life doesn't get a whole lot better than that.

Maureen slapped her knee as her thoughts exploded into words. "How about you let me give you all makeovers? I'll be like Dolly Parton in *Steel Magnolias*, and y'all just keep talking."

Hey, we were game for anything. I was certainly desperate for some beauty TLC after the shame of the bookstore experience.

So we set up the makeshift beauty parlor in the dining room, each one taking our turn to get gorgeous. Suzanne was the first to get a makeover, and we could not believe the transformation. As the wife of a pastor, Suzanne leaned toward modesty in make-up and hairstyle. She was naturally pretty, but conservative. Lots of pale pastels in her color choices. Now that Maureen had her cornered, and Suzanne was willing—our resident glamour tech-nician turned Suzanne into a raving beauty.

It was amazing for those of us who watched it take place, but the most fun of all was to follow Suzanne as she walked to a mirror to see her made-over self for the first time.

She looked in the mirror and involuntarily began to quietly shake—laughing, crying, slowly slipping down the bathroom wall until she sat, plunk, on the bathroom tile.

"I'm not supposed to be pretty," she mused with childlike wonder and sweet vulnerability. We all joined her cross-legged on the bathroom floor. It looked like a powwow for six middle-aged white women.

"Honey," Maureen said as she moved over to fix a flyaway strand of Suzanne's blond hair, "who ever told you such a thing?"

"I don't know," she answered, slightly baffled. "I just assumed I wasn't supposed to look this good. That somehow it would be drawing attention to myself."

"You look beautiful," I reassured her. "Not showy, just beautiful."

"Look at God's creation—the butterflies!" Tina reminded Suzanne. "Do you think God held back the paint when He created those things? Look at their bright colors! Look at the incredible beauty!"

By this time, somebody's well-manicured hand quietly placed a Kleenex box in the center of our grouping, for there was not a dry eye among us.

A shower of blessin' on the bathroom floor.

Tina Clark was my roommate that night. Just when we thought we were all talked out, she turned over on her side in the bed across from me, and flipped the switch on the nightstand between us.

"I was just thinkin'," she said.

"And what were you a-thinkin'?" I asked with a grin as I pulled the blankets up around my chin. How strange and wonderful it was to have bonded so closely, the six of us Southern belles, in six short hours. We'd become sisters, kindred spirits—at one point we laughingly dubbed ourselves "Big Bosom Buddies." Since I married at age seventeen, I had never experienced dorm rooms and roommates and all-night girl talk. This weekend had turned out to be a rare treat.

"I was thinking about the thing that scares me the most," Tina said, her twinkling brown eyes growing suddenly serious.

"And what is that?" I asked carefully.

"It's that I'll forget what he looked like. What his aftershave smelled like. How it felt to rub my cheek next to his stubbly chin in the mornings. How he'd sit on the kitchen bar stool and pull me close, between his knees. How I belonged there, and how nice it felt to rest my head on his chest."

Wyndell had been good, kind, and gorgeous. From his picture she carried in her wallet, he looked so rugged it was hard to imagine that something as small as a brain tumor could have taken his life. He'd lived thirty-four short years, before Tina was left, alone, to find strength to go on and raise their two sons. She'd done a magnificent job. Wyndell would have been proud of his sweet, brave, funny Magnolia.

"Tina," I said as I sat up and looked her full in the face, "you won't ever forget Wyndell! Listen to the way you talked about him just now. Your words, the way you described him, sounded like poetry. I'm about to fall in love with the guy—and I never met him!"

Tina laughed, then continued, spilling out thoughts seldom verbalized. Widows don't have many opportunities to share memories of their husbands. People have a tendency to avoid topics like tumors and bereavement and such.

"Sometimes," Tina began slowly, "I'll hear a song that

Wyndell used to play on his guitar and I can almost see his fingertips dancing on the strings and hear his voice again—that deep, wonderful voice. Songs help me remember."

"You amaze me, Tina."

"Why?"

"Because you loved Wyndell so much and you walked through the hell of his illness and death. And there you sit with love in your eyes and a smile on your face that won't quit. I don't think I've ever met a woman who is as grateful for life's little things, who lives, as they say, 'in the moment.' And you make me laugh harder than anyone I've met in the longest time. Somehow you've managed to keep your sense of humor alive and kicking. I swear, my stomach muscles are still aching from that story you told about your mother tonight."

"Oh, that one where she told her neighbor how proud she was of my brother's shiny new vulva?"

"YES!" I squealed and I was off again, laughing and holding onto the side of the bed for support.

"Oh, that's just typical Mother. She's always getting her words mixed up. Vulva, Volvo—she honestly didn't know the difference." Tina chuckled a second then grew serious again. "Becky, I don't know how to describe it—what has happened to me. But I am so happy, complete, and content—you know what I mean?"

"Okay, Tina—that's the kind of statement that boggles my mind. I mean how did you go through such awful grief and arrive at this point where life is wonderful again?"

"Oh, it's the Lord's goodness. Now don't get me wrong. I'm no saint. I have my moments of pain and loneliness. On hard days, I sometimes let a curse word or two fly. It's tough being single. Some days, I have this crazy desire to go around wearing a sign that says, 'Hey world, a great guy once loved ME.' But we were given some gifts that helped ease the pain."

"Like what?" I asked gently.

"Becky, Wyndell's sickness was often pure torture. There's nothing pretty or good about dying. But his actual death, the moment he left us, was the most beautiful thing I have ever experienced. Even more beautiful than the birth of my babies.

"His body had been paralyzed for weeks, his hands drawn up close to his chin, his eyes shut. No response to us whatsoever. But as my father and mother and I gathered around him, knowing he would be leaving us soon, Wyndell suddenly sat straight up in bed, opened his crystal blue eyes toward the ceiling—oh, Becky he had the most beautiful eyes—lifted both arms upward, then laid back in mine and my daddy's arms and died. It was obvious that something, or more accurately, *Someone* came to take Wyndell home."

Chills of holy awe went up my back.

"And then," Tina said, "after he died, a few weeks later Wyndell visited us."

"What?!"

"It happened in a dream, the most vivid I've ever had. So real, that to this day I don't believe it was just a dream. I believe it was a gift from God. When I woke up from this dream, in which my husband had held me in his arms and told me everything would be okay, I reached over to pat my Logan, who was sleeping nearby. He stirred and asked me, 'Did you see Daddy, Mom? He was here tonight. Sitting right here, in white clothes, on this bed.'

"I thought that was a little weird," Tina continued her tale as I listened intently. "I mean that we'd *both* had such vivid dreams of Wyndell, but the next morning when I went to wake Seth he could hardly wait to tell me the news.

"'Mom,' he said before I said a word, 'I know this sounds strange but Daddy came to me last night. We went scuba diving and it was *so* real! Remember how he always promised to take me? Oh man, it was too cool. I could feel the water and the waves and see the fish. I saw sharks, but Daddy said not to worry about them. It was so real.'"

"Wow," I said, shaking my head in silence as I pondered what's beyond the curtain of death. And if, as Catherine Marshall believed, God sometimes allows those whom we loved, who have gone to be with Him, to play some part in comforting us here on earth.

Tina yawned the yawn of a contented woman.

"Tired?" I asked.

"Uh-huh," she answered sleepily.

"Sweet dreams," I said without thinking.

Tina closed her eyes, smiled, and replied, "Yes, they were."

We fell asleep in God's hovering presence. Outside dewdrops fell softly in a silent benediction of blessing.

On the Fruit of Deep Sorrow

"Sometimes God calms the storm,
sometimes He lets the storm rage, and calms,
instead, the child."

—*Anonymous*

(Found on a magnet at the gift shop in Callaway Gardens)

"Where there is sorrow, there is holy ground."[1]

—*Oscar Wilde*

"Sorrow makes us all children again—destroys all
differences of intellect. The wisest know nothing."[2]

—*Ralph Waldo Emerson*

If the whole of your life had been a succession of
(calm and content) hours . . . do you know what
would have become of you? You would become
selfish, hard-hearted, lonely . . . and you would
never have felt blessedness.

When did it first dawn on you that we men
don't live unto ourselves? When did the blessedness of compassion bring comfort to you? In suffering. Where did your heart come close to those
who were so distant and cold to you? In suffering.
Where did you feel God was near to you? In suffering. Where did you first realize the blessedness of
having a Father in heaven? In suffering.[3]

—*Albert Schweitzer*

It was love at first sight.
—Susan Doran

Susan and Gregory on Christmas Eve, 1994.

Baby's Breath and Butterfly Prayers

The next morning, I awoke to the smell of coffee and herbal shampoo. Susan Doran sat at the table, her hair wrapped in a towel. She was a classic beauty, a natural blond who wore her hair in a Victorian-style upsweep (when it wasn't wrapped in a towel). Picture a model for Calgon. Suzanne had mentioned that Susan had been a flight attendant since the days the airlines called them stewardesses, and was married to a handsome pilot named Doug. I was anxious to get to know her better.

I stumbled toward the coffee-maker and filled my mug to the brim with the fragrant brew. The morning sun filtered through the miniblinds, making a striped pattern on the kitchen table. I eased into a cushioned chair with a sigh, running my hand over the surface of the wood to catch the sun's warmth on the back of my hand. What joy to awake to zero responsibilities, no agenda. Just coffee and friends. A *que será, será* kind of day, off to a slow waltzing start.

"So, Susan," I said as I struggled to connect one brain cell to the next, at least enough to form one intelligible sentence. My mind, in the mornings, is like one of those car engines that take a bit of babying to start. The first words out of my mouth are usually monosyllabic stutters, eventually followed by whole, intact, meaningful thoughts.

"Um. Uh . . . Susan. You are the only lady here I've not really had a chance to visit with yet," I finally managed to say. "Was that you and my sister I heard up until the wee hours?" I propped my sleepy head up on my palm, afraid it might fall off my neck without additional support.

"Oh, Becky," Susan said, flashing a row of perfect white teeth. "Rachel and I really hit it off last night. I feel like we've known each other forever. And we think our husbands may be twins separated at birth."

I tried to laugh, but it came out more like a sputter, my verbal engine still struggling with the warm up. I took a sip of caffeine and waited for it to take effect on my tongue. "So. Doug is a careful, detail oriented kind of a guy?" My brother-in-law, Scott St. John-Gilbert III, would make Felix Unger (the fastidious member of "The Odd Couple") seem almost laid-back.

"Oh, is he ever," Susan replied. "Cautious, like Rachel's Scott, but he and Doug both love to plan surprises too."

"Can you give me an example?" I pried, hoping Susan was up to carrying the bulk of this A.M. conversation. The best I could do was to offer a couple of questions, then sit back and serve as an interested listener.

"Well," Susan began, leaning on the table for emphasis, "you want a dramatic example?"

"Yes," I answered. "Definitely go for the drama."

"Okay," she said.

I loved the smell of a good story brewing. Next to caffeine in a cup, it's the best way to jump-start the day.

"Well, you know Doug and I married late in life, neither of us had ever had children of our own. Like most couples, I was the one with the strongest desire for a child, a longing that would not go away. After years of trying—going through the infertility nightmare of trying to have a baby with medical assistance—I had all but given up hope. I was fast approaching fifty years old at this point."

"You've got to be kidding!" I remarked, "You look so young."

"Why, thank you kindly."

"You're welcome kindly. Later I want the name of all the vitamins you take and the lotions you use. But for now, what happened next?"

"One day, out of the blue, I got a call from a social worker, Miss Martha—a friend of Suzanne's. She told me she had a little eighteen-month-old boy named Gregory who needed a home. She said, 'Susan, I honestly don't know much about him right now, but it looks like he's been diagnosed as slow, because he didn't walk until he was thirteen months old.'"

"Thirteen months?" I asked. "That's slow?"

"I know, Becky, that's what I thought, and Martha said it was a little later than normal but certainly not much. The rest of the tests done at birth were normal, if not on the high side.

"At this point in our conversation, I had to put my hand over my heart, as if to push it back into my chest. It sounded too good to be true."

"And then?"

"And then, Doug came home. I decided to broach the subject the way you hug a porcupine—*very carefully*. He was less than enthusiastic for a number of reasons. He wanted to adopt an older child since we were older parents, plus he well understood the time and attention a baby requires. As much as I wanted to plead, this was one of those decisions I dared not coerce; too much was at stake. If Doug adamantly refused, I would have to give in, and trust God to deal with my heartache."

"So what did you tell him?" I reached for a plate of toast and buttered it.

Susan handed me a jar of peach preserves. "I said, 'Look, I love you, Doug. I will always love you. You have the right to say no, and I will accept that—but as long as I've known you, you have never made a single decision without first gathering all the facts. Would you be willing to just see Gregory and meet with his foster parents and the social worker?'

"Doug agreed to the meeting, but with one condition: he had absolute veto power. I assured him he had that already."

"So you went to the meeting . . ." I took a bite of the warm sweet toast and washed it down with a sip of coffee.

"Yes, and after an encouraging meeting with the adults, Miss Martha led us to a visiting room where we were able to get down on the floor and really get to know little Gregory.

"Becky, he was so precious, so loving—free with hugs and affection, even if he was a little confused by all the new surroundings. Doug was great, laughing and playing with Gregory, completely at ease. I couldn't help but imagine the two of them gently wrestling, father and son, on our own living room floor."

"Did you both immediately know Gregory was to be yours?"

"It was love at first sight for me. In fact, it was noted in the caseworker's report that I would have taken him home that day. At the end of the meeting, we agreed to start visiting Gregory and set up several dates for those coming visits. But Doug, knowing what a life-altering event this would be, said simply, 'Susan, don't push.'"

I nodded and Susan's voice grew softer, like a storyteller building up to the best part of the tale.

"The night before our third visit with Gregory, Doug came home with a huge box, looking like a little kid with a big secret surprise. He asked me to sit down and close my eyes. I lowered myself in a chair, eyes dutifully closed, and waited.

"Finally he said, 'Okay, Susan, you can look!' And there, in the middle of the floor was a car seat. Not just any car seat. This thing was so well-equipped it could have been used in NASA space travel: bells, whistles, buttons, everything but a rocket launcher.

"But I was still afraid to get my hopes up, so I asked him, 'Doug, what does this mean?'

"'What do you *think* it means?' he asked. 'I can't let our son ride around in any old car seat.'"

"So Doug called Gregory your 'son'?" I repeated, smiling.

"Yes! Aren't those the most beautiful words? And, Becky, guess what day *our son* came home with us to stay?"

"I give up."

"Christmas Eve."

"No kidding. This sounds like one of those 'feel good' holiday movies."

"It was, really, it was. When we drove up to the foster home, Gregory's foster mother had him all bundled up in a red and green blanket, like a living Christmas present. By then, Gregory was used to us. We had quite the celebration at Doug's mother's house. The whole family was thrilled beyond belief—Gregory would be the first grandson on Doug's side."

Susan Doran had a faraway look in her eyes. From her facial expression I could see she was reliving another day, another time.

"I remember I could not take my eyes off him. He was absolutely beautiful. *Confused*—but beautiful.

"On the way home from Grandma's he fell fast asleep in the car, completely played out. The air was cool, the night dark and lovely. Before taking Gregory from the car and handing him to Doug to carry into the house, I stroked his soft hair and kissed his sweet cheeks. I wondered if there was another mother on the face of the earth as happy as I was at that moment."

"And I guess Doug felt the same?"

"Oh, my. That man is nuts about his son. And there's more to the whole 'Christmas movie' ending. For twenty-six years, Christmas had not been a wonderful day to Doug. His dad had died on Christmas afternoon, when Doug was just twenty. Doug adored his father, stayed with him and took care of him the entire last year of his father's life. Since the day his dad died, Doug's family did their best to go through the motions of celebrating

Christ's birth, but it was hard to forget sad memories of losing their husband and father.

"It was as if God sent Gregory to soothe their broken hearts with a little angel balm. With a child in the home, Christmas took on new joy and meaning again."

"There's nothing like a baby at Christmas," I agreed. "Two of my children were born in December. I had this tremendous emotional connection with how Mary must have felt as she held Jesus."

"Oh, yes, absolutely. Sometimes when I catch Gregory's eager brown eyes, the sweet softness of his cheeks, and watch my husband catch his little boy in a run-by bear hug, I just get overwhelmed with it all. God's been so good."

By the time Susan finished sharing that morning, the rest of the Georgia girls and Rachel had trickled in, one at a time, catching snippets of Gregory's sweet arrival story.

Maureen looked wistfully out the window. "I wonder if God has a child for us somewhere out there?"

Suzanne reached over and touched her friend's hand in reassurance. "I know He does, Maureen. You've got God—and Miss Martha—on your side."

Sadly, Maureen had to have an emergency hysterectomy within weeks after her wedding to Bobby, a gentle giant of a guy. They'd been married a little over two years. "Well, He's given you and Susan such wonderful little blessin's, it gives me hope."

Tina disappeared a moment, then came back to the table, holding a sack. She reached inside the paper bag, then one by one she pulled out six beautiful butterfly magnets—yellow and orange, deep blue and purple, red and black—every one unique, each brilliant in its own way.

"I bought these yesterday, one for each of us," Tina said quietly. "Before we leave this special time, I wondered if we could

each share one prayer request. Then every time we see our butterfly on our refrigerators, it will remind us to pray for each
other."

A chorus of "Thank you, Tina" and "Oh, my how sweet!" and
"Yes, let's do" started up as Tina handed us each a butterfly, then
the noise gradually came to a halt.

Maureen's full voice was the first to break the silence. "Oh,
how I'd love to be rockin' a baby this time next year."

Using her best Maureen accent, my sister said, "Now that
would be a blessin'!"

Susan added, "Maureen, you've got some praying mothers
here. No telling what God will do."

Rachel spoke next, her normally peppy voice now wavering
slightly. "Please pray for my marriage. We're going through a real
difficult time—just growing so far apart from each other emotionally." We all nodded in understanding.

Suzanne, with a newfound glow, asked that we would pray
that the Lord would help her know who she was in His eyes, "to
love who Suzanne is"—aside from the roles she plays of wife,
mother, pastor's wife.

I spoke next. "I desperately need more balance in my family
and in my work. The rush of writing is always so loud in my
head, working at home makes it hard to stop, especially when
I'm on a creative jag. I want my kids and my husband to come to
the forefront of my life, put writing and speaking and ministry
on the back burner whenever they are home."

Susan asked us to pray for Doug, who was miserable in his
work situation.

Tina asked that she would continue to sense God's nearness
and joy the way she had felt Him in the past few months. She felt
herself healing and opening to life again—five years after her
journey through grief began.

The six of us walked out of the condo into a brilliant day,
under a sky of robin's egg blue. Row after row of regal, ivory

magnolia blossoms nestled against deep green leaves. Kaleidoscopic butterflies played in the air around us. Tina paused, soaking in the wonder, then spoke for us all.

"I'm just so full, y'all." She sighed and smiled. "You know what I mean? My soul is so very *full.*"

We walked down the sidewalk toward our homebound cars, surrounded by a steady patter of chitchat, drenched with the fresh rain of God's love.

There shall be showers of blessing:
This is the promise of love;
There shall be seasons refreshing,
Sent from the Savior above.
There shall be showers of blessing—
Precious reviving again;
Over the hills and the valleys,
Sound of abundance of rain.[1]

On Friendship

"Old friends are best, unless you can find a new one fit to make an old one out of."

—*Old Saying*

"A friend is one before whom I may think out loud."[2]

—*Ralph Waldo Emerson*

"Seven years would be insufficient to make some people acquainted with each other, and seven days are more than enough for others."[3]

—*Jane Austen*

"Each friend represents a world in us, a world possibly not born until they arrive, and it is only by this meeting that a new world is born."[4]

—*Anais Nin*

"Friendship is something that raises us almost above humanity. It is the sort of love one can imagine between angels."[5]

—*C.S. Lewis*

Part 2

Magnolia
Mentors and Friends

Aren't we FUN?!
—Gracie Malone

Bluebonnet Bundle of Fun

Becky, they cut me with a knife!" Gracie Malone moaned from her bed.

"How dare they!" I empathized as I walked into the hospital room and gave Gracie a gentle hug, careful not to disturb her wound—a seven-inch long incision from her back surgery the day before. "Tell me which way those doctors went and I'll go beat them up!"

I'd dropped everything to drive nearly two hours in response to Gracie's emergency call that afternoon. Gracie is not only the designated mother hen of our writing group, which we have laughingly dubbed the Hens with Pens, she's ever the nurturer to any number of people. (As a writer's aside: when I gave this chapter to Gracie to read, she quickly pointed out that I'd inadvertently substituted the word *neuterer* for *nurturer*.)

Anyway, Gracie's call for help was unusual since she's generally the proverbial woman-in-control.

"Becky, I am so BORED," she had cried. "Nobody in this hospital has our sense of humor. I'm in a prison for dull people. Please save me. Come make me laugh."

"I'm on my way. Should I bring tacos?"

"Of course. And a . . ."

". . . Diet Coke?"

"Yes! With lots of ice."

"Gotcha. Be brave now, hang in there. Emergency rations are on their way."

Within a few days, Gracie Malone left hospital "prison" to begin her recuperation at home. I stopped by soon after, bringing lunch and a couple of books, and at Gracie's careful instructions helped her turn over on the couch every few minutes "like a chicken on a spit." But mostly, Gracie just wanted to talk and laugh. Worse than the pain of the incision for my ever-ready-to-go friend was the agony of housebound monotony.

From the start of our friendship, I could see Gracie was a woman of strong likes and dislikes. She loves blue denim, passes on froufrou. Likes chicken n' dumplings, turns her nose up at veggie plates. Would rather walk out in a field of bluebonnets and sunflowers than through a manicured garden. She's keen on having order in her own life, but thankfully, I observed how she lovingly put up with people who have all kinds of faults—from forgetfulness, to tardiness, to general all-around ditziness. The first time I met Gracie, we drove to a writer's group together in her car. The next morning Gracie noticed she was missing her notebook and several other important papers. She had phoned right away to see if I had the goods.

"Let's see," I had mused aloud, my eyes scanning the kitchen counter. "Oh dear, here they are! I must have picked them up with my purse. I'm so sorry!" Gracie laughed in response.

"Boy, am I ever relieved," I had said with a sigh.

"Why are YOU relieved?" she asked. "I'm the one who's missing the notebook with my life in it."

"I'm just glad you think this is amusing and relieved I'm still on your Potential Friend list. You may not believe this, Gracie, but there are people who actually get irate and irritable when I accidentally take their organizers or purses or keys home with me."

"Ah, no big deal, Becky. I hear kleptomaniacs make really interesting friends."

I soon realized that, with Gracie, being interesting or funny could cover any number of outright flaws. Even friends who occasionally lost their temper or tottered on the edge of sanity were often welcome in Gracie's heart and home. (I don't often lose my temper, but I have to admit, I do totter a bit.) She's as accepting and bighearted as they come as long as folks do NOT, I repeat, do NOT bore her. As long as they don't go on and on about some plain vanilla topic. Life's too short for ho-humming around—you could miss something fun. And THAT, in Gracie's book, would be tragic.

One afternoon, shortly after I absconded with her notebook, Gracie called and asked if I'd meet her for tacos and look over an article she had written. "Sure," I responded, "and you can tell me everything you know about speaking in public, since you teach Sunday school and do retreats and stuff. I've got to give a talk to a women's group next week."

"Sounds great. How's Taco Bueno sound? In, say, twenty minutes."

"Okay. You, me, nachos, and everything we both know about speaking and writing."

"Which could probably fit on one tortilla chip," Gracie quipped.

Within half an hour we were sitting in a festive booth, talkin' turkey and eating tacos as Gracie checked to make sure the three points of my talk were all theologically sound.

"So what's your article about?" I asked.

"It's about the time I tried to shed my skin," she answered nonchalantly as she reached to dip a chip into salsa.

I nearly choked on my Pepsi before sputtering, "I knew you were going to be interesting."

"Isn't that the truth? I don't even get normal sicknesses. I get fascinating diseases. You read. I'll go get us some refills."

I picked up the stack of manuscript pages and, full of curiosity, dove into her story.

Under Job's Skin
by Gracie Malone

I couldn't believe this was happening to me: my skin was coming apart at the seams.

It all began the morning I noticed a peculiar blister erupting on my chest. Within a week it was followed by a rash of watery eruptions, then black crusty sores. Eventually a huge area of open flesh covered my chest. After six weeks of tedious medical examinations, a biopsy, and several unsuccessful treatments, we finally found a doctor who knew what was wrong.

"I think you have the same illness as the Old Testament patriarch Job," he said. "It is a rare autoimmune disease. Instead of adhering, your skin cells are reacting against each other. Gracie, we'll have to treat this condition with chemotherapy drugs and steroids."

I reacted by asking two questions foremost in every sick woman's head: "How long will this take?" and "Will I lose my hair?"

As the doctor wrote out prescriptions and gave instructions for my care, he said, "Gracie, I believe you will recover, but you have to be patient. Perhaps, by the end of the year, there will be an improvement." It was August 1!

That evening Joe and I gathered our brood for a family conference. Our sons reacted with compassion. One major concern was how their outgoing mom would handle being confined at home for five months. Little did we know, that the five anticipated months was an underestimate. It would be spring before I was well again.

Every morning I went through a painful ritual of cleansing my skin, applying sterile compresses, swirling on protective cream, and carefully measuring out increasing doses of medicine. After taking the medicine, I rested in bed, avoiding even the slightest movement that would cause more pain. By afternoon the excruciating effects of the medicine subsided and I could read, watch TV, or talk with eight-year-old Jason. After dinner, Joe would help me back to bed. The nights were long, often punctuated with bad dreams.

The medicine also caused some frightening side effects. One morning I caught a glimpse of myself in the mirror: I was one odd looking bird. Lifeless tufts of hair jutted out in all directions from an almost bald head. My face was moon-shaped from steroids, my eyes sunken, my complexion a sallow gray. In addition, the large doses of cortisone produced cataracts that clouded my vision. I burst out crying.

Though I am not, by nature, prone to moodiness, I was beyond feeling blue: I was depressed. I had dedicated my life to God and thought we were friends, but when I needed Him most, I felt forgotten and alone. This dreadful feeling was worse than any physical pain! "God, why did this happen?" I asked. "Have I sinned? Are You punishing me? Do You love me?"

The next morning I propped myself up in bed with a mound of pillows, opened my Bible, and with my magnifying glass, read the words, "I have loved you with an everlasting love" (Jer. 31:3).

Today I marvel that I had the audacity to challenge the Almighty. But, I'll never forget my reaction to reading that verse. "No, You don't!" I yelled. In a fit of frustration, I grasped a handful of pages and tried to rip them out, but they were sewn in too tightly and I was too weak. I slammed the Bible on the nightstand and sobbed.

That evening I had to tell my husband the latest development. "Joe, I'm going blind. I couldn't read today without the magnifying glass." Joe knelt beside my bed and prayed, "Lord, please don't let her lose her sight. Please make Gracie well again."

Gradually my condition improved. New skin cells reproduced, covering exposed nerve endings and providing a healthy barrier against life-threatening germs. I gained strength, the depression lifted, and my attitude changed. The cataracts cleared and I could focus and read my Bible again.

As soon as I could make out words on a page, I turned to the Old Testament and located the book of Job. As I read, I felt a special kinship with him. I discovered that Job argued with God too, "Show me why You contend with me. Does it seem good to You that You should oppress?" (10:2–3 NKJV). Later, I was blessed by Job's faith, "Though He slay me, yet will I trust Him" (13:15 NKJV). I realized that God loved Job and was not punishing him. God said, "There is none like him on the earth, a blameless and upright man, one who fears God and shuns evil" (1:8 NKJV).

As I pondered these verses, a spiritual healing was taking place deep beneath my skin—in my heart. As I learned to live by faith instead of my feelings, I found rest in the shadow of God's wings.

Family members and friends became God's representatives. Our pastor provided encouragement, prayer, and books. Church members called or sent cards to cheer me. Friends took turns driving me to the doctor's office. Others helped with household chores, picked up prescriptions, and brought food.

One day Jason asked, "Mom, what are we having for supper?"

"Oh, Honey, I don't know. But you know what I wish?"
Jason shook his head, then I finished my thought. "I wish I
were well enough to cook a hot steaming bowlful of chick-
en and dumplings for you."

"And chocolate pie!" Jason added.

"Yeah!" I agreed, smacking my lips—and chocolate pie.
As soon as I'm well, Jason, as soon as I'm well.

A few hours later the doorbell rang. Unaware of our
conversation, one of my friends stood at the door, bearing
a gift in a big steaming pot—chicken and dumplings!
Before Joe could set the table, another friend arrived with
dessert. Yes, a chocolate pie.

As I took a bite of the warm dumplings, sampled the pie
and sipped coffee, I thought, You do, don't You? You do
love me with everlasting love?

Even in the midst of pain and sorrow, He is there, He
knows, He cares.[1]

"I will never leave you nor forsake you" (Hebrews 13:5
NKJV)

I looked up from the manuscript into Gracie Malone's dark
brown eyes with an odd assurance: we would be friends for a
long, long time—maybe even forever. Any woman who could
survive losing her skin and still love the Lord, reach out to others,
and find the humor in life was a woman whose shoulder I wanted
available to cry on. *Besides,* I thought, *I could really use a friend*
who loves chocolate pie.

My intuition proved right. For the past several years Gracie
and I have laughed, cried, and bonded our way into each other's
heart. Come to think of it, much of our laughing and crying and
bonding has occurred in a restaurant booth. And more than
once, we've had waitresses—even customers—stop by our table

and say, "You two look like you are having so much fun." To which we answer, "We ARE fun!"

Not long ago we were lunching in a local country-style restaurant, cutting up and chatting as usual, ideas and conversation flying at machine-gun speed. Suddenly the handsome young restaurant manager, who appeared to be Iranian, walked over to our table, looked at me and said, "Excuse me." Then he pointed to Gracie and asked, "Is she bothering you?"

I joined in the deadpan teasing without hesitation. "Yes, sir, she is."

Gracie started to open her mouth in mock protest but the man interrupted her by saying, "I'll just throw her out then. She's wasting your time and mine."

"Why are you picking on ME?" Gracie asked, incredulously.

"You look like a troublemaker, that's why," answered our friend with a wink and a grin.

As he walked away we both laughed. "What *is* it about me?" she asked.

I answered, "It's your face, Gracie. It looks like a fun face, the kind of face that invites playfulness."

From the start, Gracie Malone's been the kind of friend I can phone any time day or night, for any reason big or small. I remember calling an emergency taco meeting when I faced my first crisis with a teenager: my oldest son wouldn't comb his hair correctly—his long bangs hanging down in his face were making me crazy. Gracie reminded me that the boy under the hair was really all that mattered, and in a few years, this hair battle would fade to an amusing memory. She'd raised three sons to manhood—and, she assured me, none of them had to sling their hair out of their faces to talk or eat cereal anymore.

On one particularly overcast morning after an exhausting series of speaking trips, I called Gracie, hoping to get her to help me locate some wits. I'd misplaced mine somewhere on the last airplane trip home.

"Gracie," I sobbed, "I can't keep going. I am so, so tired and I have to drive two hours to speak in Tyler tonight and I don't know if I can make it. What can I give to others when I feel so drained and empty myself?"

"Honey," came the take-charge voice over the receiver. "Here's what we'll do. I'll drive you to Tyler. We'll have a ball. You can sleep or study or we can talk—whatever you want. Just leave the driving to me."

I didn't realize until that moment how much I needed and loved this special lady. She'd gone from my friend, Gracie Malone, to simply, *my* Gracie—a category somewhere between a friend and a nurturing mother and a crazy aunt. On the drive to Tyler, I poured out my heart, asking Gracie how to know when to say "yes" and when to say "no" to life's various requests.

"Ministry opportunities are so hard to turn down," I said, "but I don't want to be this tired again. I want to put my family first. Sometimes I wish God would just get on a loudspeaker and tell me which things are in His will and what I need to ignore."

Gracie laughed. "Oh, Hon, I know it's often tough to discern. Seems like some people have God speaking directions directly to them, because they always seem to know just what to do. Me? I have to seek Him in prayer, search the Word, and just plain use my head. He doesn't whisper the next correct move in my ear."

At this point in the conversation, Gracie pulled up to a gas station to buy some soft drinks. On the way out of the car, she paused, turned back to me, and said, "If you do good on your speech, I might take you for coffee and dessert afterwards."

"Okay, but maybe we'd better pray about it first and see if it's God's will," I teased.

Gracie closed her eyes reverently for half a second, then opened them quickly. "God said, 'Yes, definitely have pie.'"

"Gracie, you are so BAD!" I exclaimed with a grin. Then I leaned back and sighed as I closed my eyes and mumbled. "But at least you're not boring."

She left a trail of laughter as she disappeared into the store. The evening I had been dreading turned out to be a rare delight. Thanks to one wacky, nurturing friend.

Tonight I received a surprise call. News from Gracie I didn't want to hear.

"Becky, I'm back in the hospital."

"What?!?"

"I know. Can I complicate my life, or what? The doctors say I'm leaking sap or something from my back." She tried to be lighthearted, but I can detect Gracie's mood by her first 'hello.'

"Gracie, what's going on, really?"

"Becky, they did an MRI, and it showed I have a staph infection where I had my surgery. I'm scared spitless. They are going to open me up again and wash out all the bad stuff, then sew me up again."

"Oh, Gracie. Not again! Can't we hens just run you through a car wash?!?"

"I wish . . . Becky. I know God is in control, but I need your prayers. I'm really getting weary . . ." Her voice had that pitiful trying-to-be-brave sound to it. It reminded me of how my son, Zeke, would talk to himself when he was about seven or eight, trying to shore up his emotional strength before going into the doctor's office for a vaccination.

"I'm so sorry, Gracie. You know I will pray."

"Thank you, Becky. And there's something else."

"What?"

"I was supposed to speak at a conference this weekend. Four one-hour talks on Friday and Saturday. And I was wondering if . . ."

". . . I could impersonate you?"

"Well, yes. Just act a little bossier and more in control than you normally do. Don't lose your keys or run late or wear your dress inside out. That would give it away. They'd know it was you . . ."

"Look Gracie, if you will promise to get better, I'll go speak to 100 strangers this weekend and try to be you. But I can't guarantee I won't lose anything. That's a gamble you'll just have to take—and seeing that you are flat on your wounded back, you are in no position to negotiate."

"We are fun, aren't we?"

"Yes, Gracie, we are fun." I paused before adding, "We are CRAZY. But we are fun."

"I love you, Hon."

"And I love you too," I said.

"Call me when you get back in town?"

"Yes. And I'll bring . . ."

". . . tacos?"

"Of course. And a Diet Coke. And—if you are very, very good . . ." I added.

"Chocolate pie?"

"I don't know, I might have to pray about that one."

There was a short pause on the phone and then Gracie's voice grew stronger, with that familiar take-charge tone I'd grown to love. "I just asked God and He said to tell you, 'Bring pie.'"

Now I ask you, how could I argue with that?

That night I prayed, *Father, watch over my Gracie tonight. Guide the surgeons tomorrow as they work on her back. I love her, Lord. I want to hear her laughter for lots of years to come. I would love Gracie to be able to enjoy long walks again, without fighting back tears and pain. I want her to sit across from me and spout writing ideas and eat fast-food again. Please heal her. Quickly. (You know how she does like speedy results.) And one more important request, Dear Lord: Please, please don't let her get BORED.*

I am pleased to report the surgeons caught the infection before it did any permanent damage, and within a few days sent Gracie home to recover—with IV bottles and a home health nurse, just to be on the safe side.

On Having Fun

"A good and wholesome thing is a little harmless fun in this world; it tones a body up and keeps him human and prevents him from souring."[2]

—*Mark Twain*

"Among those whom I like or admire, I can find no common denominator, but among those whom I love, I can: all of them make me laugh."[3]

—*W.H. Auden*

"Humor is a prelude to faith, and laughter is the beginning of prayer."[4]

—*Reinhold Niebuhr*

"Don't take yourself too seriously. And don't be too serious about not taking yourself too seriously."[5]

—*Howard Ogden*

Life begins at 80!
—Vivian Birdwell, 87

7

Youthful Bird of Paradise

Gracie Malone knocked at the front door, then entered with a curtsy and a grin.

In spite of the rain that was coming down in sheets, Gracie's hair looked great, her makeup flawless. She was decked out in her favorite denim dress, adorned with classy silver jewelry. The entire ensemble was accentuated by a lovely IV bottle, which she held in her right palm. A tube led to a vein in her inner arm. She gripped a syringe of saline solution with her left hand, hoisting it up as if it were the Statue of Liberty's torch.

"Not bad for an invalid, eh?" she asked, raising her eyebrows in expectation of praise. She didn't have to wait long, as I stood ready, loaded with "attagirls" and "way to gos."

Gracie, *my* Gracie, was getting back to her old self after more than ten weeks (and counting) of recovery from her second back surgery. Except for her portable medical accessories—antibiotics that had to be given intravenously twice a day—she was up and driving and ready for fun.

The adventure *du jour*? We were off to visit an octogenarian.

I met Vivian Birdwell, eighty-seven years young, at a speaking engagement this past spring. Even as I told stories from the platform, I felt drawn to her aqua eyes, sparkling with goodwill and sprinkled with mischief. She reminded me of a small scarlet bird; on her tiny frame she wore a bright red dress, draped with a classic white shawl. Throughout my talk, Vivian maintained rapt eye contact, her white hair bobbing joyously as she laughed. She appeared to be having a remarkably good time. Once the evening wound down and most good-byes were said, I lingered, chatting with Vivian in the church hallway. At evening's end, I knew this lady was special, a rare ruby among women.

"Listen, life begins at eighty! Oh, I just had an idea: you've got to come out and see me some Tuesday." Vivian exclaimed, spreading wide her arms. "We'll visit in the morning, then zip out for a fast-food lunch. Then we'll come back to my house, and I'll introduce you to the ladies of our 'Let's Be Friends' group. It's a club we started for widows, but we're open to anybody who's lonely. We don't serve refreshments, don't take a collection, and there's no such thing as coming too early or staying too late. There's no agenda and no rules, except 'no gossip.' Oh, and our mottoes are: 'I can't remember' and 'I forgot.'"

I eagerly accepted Vivian's invitation. When I mentioned my plans to Gracie, she enthusiastically agreed to come along, even volunteering to chauffeur.

"Vivian lives in a little town called Chandler, just west of Tyler," I explained to Gracie as I sipped a to-go cup of coffee and fumbled with a page of my handwritten, hieroglyphic directions. "We should be seeing a sign pretty soon."

"Population 1,600," Gracie read aloud, spying the Chandler city limits sign as she navigated the car through the rain.

"My directions say 'Turn left at the Assembly of God, then left at the Church of Christ until you come to the red cardinal in the front yard.'"

"Cardinal?"

"That's what she said," I answered with a shrug.

We followed the directions and, sure enough, pulled up in front of a house with the red cardinal flying out front—a red cardinal-shaped *flag*, that is.

Vivian Birdwell was at the front door, waving us in from the weather, talking before we even exited the car. I'd learned that Vivian's pastor calls her the Mother Theresa of Chandler. We were about to discover why.

"Now before you even say a word," Vivian began, "I want to invite you to spend the night after the 'Let's Be Friends Club' meeting. I've got two guest rooms, a bathroom and two unused toothbrushes."

Gracie and I declined amid some protest, then proceeded to follow this cheerful, elfin lady on a tour of her home.

First exhibit: family pictures.

"This is my Walter," she said lovingly, pointing to a picture of a man who could have been Vivian's twin—except that he was six feet tall, and, well, we'd have to really stretch Vivian to get her to measure a full five feet. (As limber as she is, she might be game to let us try.) The picture was of the Birdwells' fiftieth anniversary; Walter went on to heaven ahead of Vivian about five years after the pose was taken.

The pair in the portrait had narrow faces, laughing eyes, impish smiles, and wonderful wrinkles, like folds of softly draped silk—tokens of their many years together. Vivian wore her snow white hair in a long braid wrapped around the top of her head, Swedish style. Her soft skin was faintly rouged and powdered. On the special occasion of their anniversary, she wore a dress of blue calico with a wide crocheted collar. Walter sported a handsome blue suit and tie.

Moving on down the wall, we met eight-by-tens of her two grown sons and their wives.

"Tom and Kim moved me down here from Kansas City three years ago, right after Walter died. Fixed up this house for me so all I had to do was walk in the door and start living. Kim has a gift for decorating and bought many of the special touches. Even had my clothes all hung up in the closet." Vivian paused, her hand on the picture but her face turned up to meet my eyes. She giggled, not a chuckle, not a laugh, but the most charming, infectious little girl giggle. "They were worried I might be bored and lonely!"

I laughed in response, and Vivian slapped her knee. Gracie hadn't stopped grinning since the minute she walked in my kitchen that morning—still euphoric to be out and about again.

Vivian pointed to the second picture. "My son, Walt, is named for his father, of course—and this is his lovely wife, Yolanda." Walt and Tom both sported silvery beards, and I asked Vivian if they were born with them—mostly so I could hear that great giggle again.

"Look here, what Yolanda gave me." Vivian lifted a stuffed bear from a shelf. It wore a shirt embroidered with three letters, "LMS."

"What does the LMS stand for?"

"Los Mejores Suegros," Vivian answered in flawless Spanish. "It means 'the very best in-laws.' Yolanda is Hispanic, and so special to me. She speaks perfect English, but I wanted to speak to her in her native language. So, about thirty years ago—I guess I was about fifty-seven years old—I took Spanish lessons. I order my *Reader's Digest* and *The Americas* magazines in Spanish because I love reading the language."

I was amazed at Vivian Birdwell's sharp mind, and chagrined to realize that she was smarter than me! Her casual reading would intimidate some Ph.D.s—but there was never a hint of boasting about this bright lady. She simply had a natural lust for life, her thirst for learning springing from a Curious George-like personality. "With so little time to spare these days, I want to read something that will either amuse or inform me," she stated matter-of-factly. Gracie and I both noted the presence of a small, leather Spanish-English dictionary on the bathroom counter, in a place where most women tuck *Woman's Day* and *Good Housekeeping*."

One of her favorite books is by Spanish author Emilio Rojas, called *Little Friend (Pequeño Hombre)*, also a gift from Yolanda. Though it sounds like a children's book, it is not. Vivian read one of the short stories aloud (without reading glasses), never missing a beat or struggling to make out the tiny words.

"I love this collection because they read like mythical stories, but they are really philosophical essays," Vivian said. "They make you think."

Vivian Birdwell's house was as cozy as you'd dream a grandmother's house should be—lots of slipcovered couches, dotted with keepsakes, like tiny spoons from faraway places and heirloom plates. A wash-and-wear "guardian angel" of white cotton and lace stood guard above her bed. With childlike delight, Vivian lifted the angel's soft dress to show off its lace pantaloon. In nearly every room there was some sort of painted or hand-stitched scene of a red cardinal.

"I've always loved cardinals," Vivian explained. "And yellow roses. When I was a little girl, every year on my birthday, I'd get a yellow rose from my neighbor's front yard. I guarded it like a jewel, cupping its petals in my hands and holding it against my little chest, afraid someone might take it or a breeze might blow away its petals."

Yes, this is the kind of colorful woman who'd love red birds and yellow roses.

We readied ourselves to head out for lunch—grabbing purses, turning off lights—careful to avoid tripping over Vivian's tiny trampoline. I was grateful Vivian had chosen fast-food for lunch—spicy Mexican food, no less—over blue-haired lady cafeteria fare.

On the way down the hall to the front door, Vivian told us she had recently broken her arm. "The doctor gave me a hot pink cast, and when I asked him why he chose pink, he said, 'White is for boring people—and you don't qualify.'"

At this point Gracie discreetly asked me if I ought to offer to help Vivian into the car. "Why?" I replied in a whisper. "She's practically skipping. And . . ." I pointed to Vivian as she passed by in a whirl, ". . . she's gaining on both of us."

Vivian Birdwell entertained us on the short drive with tales of moving to her neighborhood three short years before. "When the neighbors heard that Tom's eighty-four-year-old mother was moving into the house, one of them asked, 'Is she active?' It took Tom a while to stop laughing so he could answer them. The first Sunday I was here, a couple of people from church came to serve me communion at home. I thanked 'em kindly and offered to do the same for them sometime."

We chuckled and then Gracie asked, "What do you do in a typical week, Vivian?"

"Well, let's see. Every Tuesday and Thursday afternoon I help with the Kid's Club—an after-school program at our church. It's for latchkey kids. Once a month I help out with God's Open Hand—a ministry and store for people who are struggling financially. Tomorrow, there's Meals on Wheels—"

"You mean they bring you a meal?" Gracie asked.

"No," Vivian looked up, a little surprised. "I take the meals to the elderly." It was a slow dawning, but the dawning came. Vivian did not see herself as one of the "elderly," thank you very much. As a matter of fact, Gracie and I both felt older and more fatigued than this wisp of a whippersnapper disguised as a cute little old lady.

"I'm also a member of the United Methodist women's group. Now I did quit the Hobby Club because they do fundraisers—bake sales. Everyone bought Pauline's famous Italian cream cake and Aylne's pecan pie. After I bought back my own dessert twice, I decided my talents could be better used elsewhere. So now I'm on the board of the Lioness Club. I modeled my red dress in the Lioness style show!"

Her mention of the Lioness Club made me smile as my mind rabbit trailed to the first time I ever spoke to a meeting of a local Lion's Club. To my surprise, every member introduced themselves with the surname "lion": as in "Lion George" or "Lion Bill" or "Lion John." I'd managed to stifle my giggles until one of the men gravely introduced himself as "Lion Leo"—and I lost it.

As Gracie wheeled us into Taco Bell's parking lot, I snapped back to the moment. Again, Vivian beat both of us to the door and held it open for us so we could duck out of the rain.

"What vitamins do you think she takes?" I asked Gracie over my shoulder.

"I don't know," came her fast reply, "but I want some of whatever she's having."

Once we received our orders, we snuggled into a corner booth. The restaurant was alive with color—bright purples and reds and canary yellows, colors one would find in a dazzling bird of paradise flower in a tropical paradise. The decor reflected our festive mood. As the rain fell softly outside, a tree frog attached itself to the window near us.

"We've got company," Vivian remarked, glancing toward the frog.

Most rainy days seem so gloomy to me. This one, I noted, did not. The drip-drop of the autumn shower only added to the coziness of our gathering. I fancied us as three generations of women happily huddled in a rainforest hut—only instead of gnawing at roasted wild boar, we were eating paper-wrapped tacos and drinking colas from a straw. "So Vivian," I said, "I'd love to hear how you and Walter fell in love."

"Oh, that's a fun story," she began, holding her soft taco in midair. "We only had two dates before we got married. But they were long ones. The first one began in the hospital where I was a nurse. Walter came in as a patient with a ruptured disc. I liked him right off, so I tied a ten-pound weight on his feet and wouldn't let him go."

We listened in fascination as the true story unfolded. The attraction, we learned, had been mutual. Before Walter even exited the hospital, he'd asked Vivian to marry him.

"But I told him lots of patients fall in love with their nurses, so we'd just wait and see."

When Walter asked Vivian for a date the first week he was out of the hospital, she let her hopes rise. They spent their first date picnicking with her family, but later that evening Walter took the smitten Vivian, alone, to a movie. They talked effortlessly, as if they'd always known one another. Walter discovered that the next day would be Vivian's birthday and sent her a gorgeous bouquet of flowers: a dozen yellow roses. That sealed it for Vivian: this was love.

It wasn't long before Walter telephoned again, asking if Vivian would be interested in a second date.

"I'd love to see you, Walter," she had answered weakly, "but I'm feeling horrible." By evening's end, Vivian entered the hospital with a 103-degree temperature and immediately had surgery for pneumococcic peritonitis, a staph-like infection that had taken the lives of two doctor's wives within the last six weeks. The doctors gravely told young Walter, "Son, we can only give her one chance in a hundred to live." In the preantibiotic days, sulfa drugs were the only recourse—and sorely inadequate for this major infection.

"When I woke up from surgery," Vivian recounted, "Walter was there, and I knew I would live. I had too much to live *for*. As long as he held my hand, I was able to get some sleep." In his vigilant watching and worrying over Vivian, Walter completely lost his appetite. The kindhearted owners of the hotel where he was staying (to be closer to the hospital) placed fresh bottles of milk at Walter's doorstep each day, hoping he would drink something for nourishment.

Eventually Vivian recovered fully. She and Walter quickly married each other—before one of them dared get sick again. They said their vows in a log home on the family land where Walter's grandmother had been born. Before she left the hospital, Vivian's doctor had warned her to wait for his "okay" before marrying Walter, for her health's sake. But the young lovers weren't about to wait for permission.

"When I walked back into the doctor's office for my check-up," Vivian said, mischief dancing in her eyes, "he took one look at me and asked, 'When did you get married?' I guess our secret showed in the happiness on my face.

"There were two things Walter and I agreed on before we got married. First of all we promised to always show each other respect. The other was that we would take care of each other's parents when they could no longer care for themselves. And so, it happened that my mother and father, and Walter's mother came to live with us—all in the same year."

"Oh, my!" I exclaimed, trying to imagine going from newly-weds to an instant family of five—three members being in-laws! "How long did your parents live?"

"My mother lived for seven years after she and Daddy moved in. She loved Walter so much, every day she'd ask me when he was coming home. He'd bring her a pint of ice cream, you see. Daddy was a kindhearted man, a Methodist missionary, determined to live long enough to take care of Mother. Three weeks after Mother died, my father took a nap in a chair and never woke up, his job on earth completed. Walter's mother, Granny Fanny, lived with us seventeen more years—twenty-four years in all."

"Wow," Gracie spoke for both of us, "did you two ever have any privacy?"

"Not much. We managed to have two sons," (here Vivian winked) "but even that took some doing. At any time one of our folks might knock at the bedroom door. And Granny Fanny, bless her heart, never knew the meaning of the word *tact*. Now she was a case!"

"With a name like Granny Fanny, you've got to have stories about her," I encouraged.

"Oh, my, yes. One night our friends, Leo and Myrtle, telephoned to see if we wanted them to come over for a game of pinochle. Granny Fanny answered the phone saying, 'Well, Vivian and Walter said you might call, but said they really don't care whether you come or not.' When our resilient company arrived and we were happily playing the game, Granny Fanny leaned over to Leo, who was eating a piece of pie, and said, 'I was going to eat that for breakfast, but look what you've gone and done.' She was a mess."

"How did you put up with her for twenty-four YEARS?" Gracie and I asked in near unison.

"It never occurred to me not to. She was a part of the family. But I did long to get away sometimes. It didn't happen often. We hired someone to come watch Granny Fanny once—after she'd lived with us about three years—just so we could go out for the evening alone. When we came home she said, 'Well I guess that was all right, but I wouldn't make a habit of it.'

"She loved to go places with me in the car, but she repeated the same tired old phrase every time she'd get in the front seat. She'd say, 'I've been over this same road a thousand times.' I knew Granny wanted variety, but, you know, there are only so many ways to the grocery store. One day she started in with, 'I've been over this road . . .' and I stopped the car, turned it around, and drove her back home.

"The next time we drove to the store she was quiet as a mouse all the way there, but on the way back, about three blocks from the house, she began again. 'I've been over this road a thousand times . . .' I gave her a look that could knock over a mule, and she quickly added, 'but it sure beats nothin''

Gracie and I shook our heads, smiling. Vivian took a bite of her taco.

"You gals want some coffee?" Gracie offered. Vivian and I nodded.

While Gracie was gone, and Vivian finished up her lunch, I was momentarily lost in my own thoughts. *How do you survive the loss of your parents and ultimately, the loss of the man you've loved for fifty-five years? How do you go on?* When Gracie came back with our coffees, I voiced these questions aloud.

"Though I loved Walter as much as humanly possible, I had to accept that my life with him was finished. I had to say to myself, 'That was one life, Vivian, now you must build a new one. That was Act I, now it's time for Act II.'

"Walter lived through two heart attacks. He had four bypasses one year, and during surgery one of the bypasses broke loose and we nearly lost him again. Several years later, surgeons put in a pig's valve; Walter used to tease that he always fought an urge to 'oink' when he saw corn.

"After the second major surgery, I took him home thinking we'd slow our pace a bit. But he'd have none of that. 'Vivian,' he said, 'I'm not running scared. I'm much more concerned about the quality of my life than the quantity.' So off we went on mountain trips, fishing in Montana, camping . . ."

"How many years did you have with him after the second surgery?"

"Sixteen. Sixteen glorious years. Walter asked to be cremated when he died. Some of his ashes are in my front yard. The rest we divided up in vials and gave to our sons and Walter's hunting buddies. After a memorial campfire, each hunter took a vial of Walter's ashes and sprinkled them on their favorite hunting spot."

How good to have lived so boldly, to be remembered in fond places.

"What about the grief?" I asked. "Was it just awful?"

"Oh, yes, it was hard. But I learned a lot about not running scared from Walter. There's a quote I love, 'Not everything ends with death. I have only gone to the next room.' Walter did not cease to exist, only his body is gone. I'll see him again. I think of him as being as close as the next room.

"Because I moved through the grief process fairly well, my minister here asked me to reach out to other widows. One of the things most widows do is talk about how much they miss their husbands, how their lives have changed, how much their mates suffered. I think listening is one thing I do fairly well, so for a good while I sit quietly and let them talk it all out. If I were to be remembered for one quality, I hope it would be for 'empathy.'

"After a while I'll say, 'Now let's remember the happy things.' If we choose to remember the good things about our life and our happy days as a couple, we find more strength to go on."

I checked my watch. "Hey, girls, it's almost 1:30. We'd better get back to Vivian's house before the friends arrive."

When we pulled up in front of the house with the red cardinal, Vivian instructed us to park a ways down the street. "We have to leave the driveway open for the ones with wheelchairs coming from the nursing home. First time we put on this little gathering, there were so many cars parked out front, the neighborhood thought I'd died."

And then the parade began. One by one, adorable ladies filed in: Esther, Bobbie and Bettye and Brenda and Beth, Louise and Lois, Oleta and Marita, Dortha and Dorothy, Josie and Jean, Ellen and finally, Frances. Brenda, Vivian's coconspirator in this friendship venture, gaily introduced herself as a junkie and hooker. "I collect junk and hook rugs," she hastened to explain.

Dorothy came down the hall, pushing her walker in front of her. She had arrived from the nursing home—which she told us had an outbreak of the epazooties.

"What's epazooties?" I asked.

"Don't know," answers Dorothy, nodding her head knowingly. "They won't tell us."

It was Dorothy's birthday. She was eighty-six years old that day, so Marita hopped up and serenaded her with an original, impromptu birthday song. A slow smile spread over Dorothy's face as she commented with genuine surprise. "I used to think seventy-four sounded ancient. Now it sounds like a youngster's age."

Brenda said, "I don't feel old at all. Of course the other day my baby called and told me he got a set of dentures and that made me pause to think."

Vivian was right. There was absolutely no order or agenda to this whole "Let's Be Friends" affair. There were four or five conversations going on at once. The only frustration for me was I couldn't decide which interesting conversation to join. One group was remembering how things were in the old days, how they never said words like *PMS* or *pregnant* aloud.

"Why, remember when it came around to our time of the month, we used to go to bed?"

"That's right," bobbed another gray head in agreement. "It was our sick time."

"And we wouldn't dare wash our hair or take a bath at that time. We thought we'd die!"

Another group was laughing about a women's club which "flocked" its citizens—setting out ten or twenty ugly plastic pink flamingos in some poor soul's yard, then forcing the victim to pay the club in order to have them removed. "It's a terrific little fund-raiser," one lady chimed in brightly. Every so often, someone read a piece of poetry or a short story from a book.

All the "Let's Be Friends" ladies were funny and charming, but the group agreed that Vivian was the belle of their weekly ball.

"She's all heart, she really is."

"Never know what she's going to do next."

"We're afraid to skip a meeting, or we'll miss a Vivian story."

"Vivian, tell Becky and Gracie about the wedding you went to a few weeks ago."

"Oh, that was so much fun," Vivian obliged. "I went up early to Lake Latawanna in Missouri to help out, and for three days none of us were allowed in the kitchen—for fear the wedding cake would fall. The bride, Melanie, is like a granddaughter to me. She's an astronomer and, Becky, she's an author too. She's written some science books that have been translated in nine languages! Oh, listen—in the front of one of them is a real embarrassing misprint. It was supposed to say she worked at the 'Public Observatory.' But they left the 'l' out of 'public.'"

After the laughter and comments died down, Vivian picked up the story again. "The groom is a NASA engineer. He's going to be in charge of the next Mars shot. They met at a juggling club. They've even juggled on national TV!

"The couple married under a big oak tree, and after they said 'I do,' they turned to face us, one arm around each other and juggled some Indian clubs with their two free hands. Instead of throwing rice, we got to shoot them with water pistols. Then the groom's brother announced he had to leave to go climb a mountain in Chile. They're a real adventurous sort."

At this point, I was imagining a wedding performed by Barnum and Bailey, but Vivian hastened to tell me it was not. It was fun, but really beautiful and romantic, full of loving commitment.

"The wedding invitation said to bring bathing suits so of course, I did. Then Bob, the bride's father, asked me if I wanted to ride a Sea-Doo. I said, 'You bet!' and the next thing I knew I was sitting behind Bob doing doughnuts in the lake on the back of a jet ski. It was more fun! One time Bob looked back to check on me. The front end of the Sea-Doo was sticking up out of the water and we were really moving. You know what I said when he asked if I was okay?"

"WHAT?" we all asked at once.

Vivian's eyes grew wide with childlike excitement. "I said, 'WHEEEEEEEEEEEEEEEEEEEEEE!'"

Gracie Malone and I hated to leave this fun "girls' day out" party. The only difference between this company of women and the chick gatherings I've been to before is that some of these gals pushed walkers or rode wheelchairs, while my friends struggled with diaper bags and strollers. Also, there was less hurry and more of a tendency to linger and enjoy. I thought of the child who once lovingly wrote, "Grandmas are the only people who have TIME."

Before we said our good-byes, the gals gave Gracie and me each a book of the inspirational thoughts they'd been collecting for three years, since the month Vivian Birdwell flew into Chandler and began livening things up.

I leafed through the homemade booklet and right away, one of the pieces reminded me of Vivian Birdwell.

"Your Grandma's seventy," our father said,
"So mind your manners when she comes to stay with us.
No quarreling. No rowdy play. She's old and frail."
And all we felt was dread.
But when she came she took us by surprise—
Beat us at checkers, dominoes, and walked the farm's length,
Picnicked on a stump and talked
To our pure joy, with laughter in her eyes.
The day she left we cried, because we knew
Grown-ups as young as Grandma were so few.
By Helen Mitchel, shared by Bonnie Farmer

Just as Vivian's beloved red cardinals cheer the landscape with their tiny bursts of brilliant color, so Vivian Birdwell continues to color her world with youthful ways and welcoming smiles.

May she live long enough to spread plenty of joy, but not so long she actually grows up!

On Wisdom, Widowhood, and the Will to Live Long

Not everything ends with death. I have only gone to the next room. All that we have been to each other we still are. Laugh as we have always laughed at the little jokes we enjoyed together . . .

Let my name continue to be the familiar word that it always was. I shall only be waiting for you, someplace very near here, just around the corner.

—Conan Scott Holland, from "Facts of the Faith,"
shared by Vivian

I have good news for you. The first eighty years are the hardest. The second eighty are a succession of birthday parties.

Being eighty is a lot better than being seventy. At seventy, people are mad at you for everything. At eighty, you have a perfect excuse no matter what you do. Everyone is looking for symptoms of softening of the brain.

If you survive until you are eighty, everybody is surprised that you are still alive. They treat you with respect just for having lived so long . . .

If you ask me, life begins at eighty!

—Author unknown

There was no audible voice from heaven . . .
I just knew He was there.
—Brenda Waggoner

8

Morning Glory of Grace

I was driving my twelve-year-old son, Gabe, home from football practice one night. He was unusually quiet, so I asked him, "What are you thinking about?"

He laughed, then blurted out, "French fries!" He pulled his shoulder pads out of his jersey, then looked over at me and asked, "What are you thinking about?"

I told him I was thinking of one of my best friends: Brenda Waggoner.

"I like her," he said sincerely.

"She's special, isn't she?"

Gabe nodded with enthusiasm. Twelve-year-old boys are like those dogs in the movies that can sense real goodness in a person. Kids tend to tell the unedited truth about grown-ups. And Gabe knows what I know. What everyone who meets and loves Brenda Waggoner knows. There's something amazing about this woman. But what, exactly, is it?

"I want to write about Brenda tonight," I explained to my son as we drove along the glistening lake to our home. "But there's a problem. I need to pick one quality about her—one thing that makes Brenda unique."

"There are too many good things, aren't there?"

"Yes." I smiled at my son before turning my gaze out the window. The sun was stretching its blazing fingers, bronzing the earth before taking its leave. "Too many good things."

Back home in the kitchen I cornered my husband between the counter and the refrigerator and caught him in a hug. Then I turned to pour a cup of coffee into my favorite china pedestal mug. "Scott, I want to ask you something."

"Sure," my husband answered, pulling a bar stool to the counter and taking a seat. "Shoot."

"Okay, here's the deal. We both love Brenda. She's as much your friend as mine—so tell me: what would you say makes her special?"

"She *feels*," he said without hesitation.

I grinned at Scott's answer, but immediately grasped his meaning. "You are exactly right. But I can't just write down 'Brenda *feels*.' It sounds strange."

"But it is what she *does*. She feels what others are going through. It's like she's 'perceptively sensitive.'"

"Yeah," I mused. "Perceptively sensitive."

"And she's open and vulnerable," Scott added.

"And so wise."

"But childlike," Scott countered.

"She's compassionate," I reminded him.

"And passionate about life."

"Yes—and wouldn't you say, 'uninhibited?'"

Scott nodded. "And kind and creative and caring."

"She's just *Brenda*," I said softly.

"She's Brenda," Scott agreed with a what-else-can-we-say? shrug.

Like most women who first viewed the delightful movie, *Anne of Green Gables*, or read the book as a young girl, I identified with

Anne Shirley's longing for a special friend. Not just any friend but the kind one searches for all our life: "a kindred spirit and a bosom buddy." I've had lots of friends—close, valued friends. But in my most honest moments, I knew I had not yet found a true kindred spirit and bosom buddy. Perhaps she was not to be found. *Anne of Green Gables* was, after all, a fictitious story.

Who would have guessed that I'd eventually find the friend I'd waited for all my life right in front of my eyes. And who'd have dreamed she'd turn out to be a professional therapist?

Brenda Waggoner appeared to me to epitomize the word *together*. She had the willowy body of a dancer and on Sunday mornings she often wore well-tailored suits in brilliant hues of scarlet, deep turquoise, or soft pink. Her dark hair, streaked with silver, was cut in classic Cleopatra style and though I admired Brenda's stylish look from a distance, it never crossed my mind that we'd become more than nodding acquaintances. Brenda had raised her children. She was a career woman. She was *mature.*

I, on the other hand, could nearly always be found running into church late, attaching an earring or pinning on a wayward button or painting over a run in my hose with fingernail polish. I was in the middle of a crazy life few could fathom. And to make matters worse, I'd landed in a church of left-brain parishioners. A group of folks who hugged their organizers only slightly less tightly than their Bibles and concordances and precept study outlines.

In contrast, I was an out-of-shape, artsy, humor writer—a mother of four living in a cabin on a lake, trying to relate to women who often reminded me of a batch of Barbie Dream Moms. I couldn't help notice that their Bible study answers were actually written in the spaces provided, rather than at long slants, or around the edges of the paper with curlicues and loopy embellishments, as my musings were. Try as I might, I just couldn't fit the standard profile of a church lady. *Brenda Waggoner, on the other hand,* I thought, *now she's the type that will fit here perfectly.*

And so it came as a great surprise when Brenda called one day and invited me over for lunch. It was a rainy autumn morning when I set out for her house, driving up and down endless gravel roads and turns to a wooded spot in the country. I'd been shocked to learn that Brenda and her husband, Frank, didn't live in a ritzy neighborhood, but resided, instead, in a small town with the hick-sounding name of Farmersville. When I drove up to Brenda's home I was secretly delighted to find it was no Barbie Dreamhouse, but more of a *Little House on the Prairie* affair, with a welcoming pair of rocking chairs on its friendly front porch.

When Brenda opened the door and invited me inside I felt almost as if I were walking into the wardrobe from C.S. Lewis's children's tale, and coming out in Narnia. Brenda wore her "comfy clothes" today—and she looked surprisingly young. Over her stretch jeans, made of a whimsical rose-printed fabric, she wore an oversize pink sweater, with the sleeves pushed up on her elbows.

"Come in! I'm so EXCITED you are here!" she said, arms open wide—and I'm not making this up or giving in to literary exaggeration—with *glee*. "Wait until you see my favorite room!"

Brenda Waggoner, classy lady, professional counselor—had transformed before my eyes into a little girl bursting with excitement over this occasion she'd obviously been anticipating with delight. To say the least, I was touched.

As I followed Brenda through the living room, my senses were tempted with smells of freshly baked pecan pie, potpourri, and hazelnut coffee. I could see birds flitting among the branches of the red and gold leaves outside an enormous picture window. A fire was glowing, yes, in the hearth. And somewhere over and above me a flute was playing one of my favorite songs from *The Phantom of the Opera*—"All I Ask of You." (I assume it was from a stereo and not a real flutist hidden in the rafters, but I cannot say that for certain.)

Brenda explained that her husband Frank had built this

delightful home, and then invited me to take a peek at her favorite room. Everywhere I looked were touches of girlhood: old dolls and pictures from years gone by, ribbons and lace, tiny dresses and shoes, stuffed bears, wooden toys, beloved children's books, and diminutive furniture. With pride, she showed me a little handmade book—a gift from one of her small friends, a little neighborhood boy of about six.

"Don't you love the words he uses?" Brenda asked, as she lovingly ran her fingers under the child's lopsided lettering.

"Yes, they're wonderful," I agreed and then asked. "Do you write or keep a journal?"

"Yes, I've always written my thoughts, as long as I can remember," Brenda answered.

"May I see some of them?"

"I'd love that, if you wouldn't mind."

We journeyed to the kitchen and sat at a handmade table that Frank had made. Soon Brenda appeared with a leatherbound notebook full of her treasures: poetry, heartfelt journaling, stories, and faded photos.

"Did you know Frank is my second husband?" she asked quietly. I shook my head. Frank and Brenda were such a great match, such a loving couple, that it was hard to imagine Brenda could have ever been married to anyone else. "Yes," she sighed, "I went through a painful divorce almost seventeen years ago."

"Can you tell me about it?"

Brenda unfolded the tale, probably a sadly familiar one to many women who've experienced the death blow to their wedding vows.

Brenda described how she became a Christian in her mid-thirties, full of zeal and ready to tackle the wonderful plan she thought God had for her life. She never dreamed the day would come when she'd hear her husband of fifteen years announce he was leaving. The pain of his announcement was compounded by the discovery that he had been unfaithful. They also had two young sons who suffered from inevitable fallout of divorce. All Brenda's valiant attempts to be the perfect Christian wife had shattered at her feet. Her beloved family, rent in two.

"I can't even imagine how much that must have hurt," I commented, shaking my head slowly.

"I was the classic cheerleader who married the football star. We had created this neatly packaged happy suburban life," Brenda explained. "Then suddenly it was all over, and I had no idea what to do next. Writing down thoughts in my journal was a source of continuing solace during those dark times. One by one, God used this horrible, lonely time to break down the prison of my own perfectionism. Eventually, He began pouring out grace in its place."

It came as no surprise to me that Brenda identified so strongly with Henri Nouwen's image of *The Wounded Healer*. As we visited, she shared a quote from her worn copy of Nouwen's book:

> *Nothing can be written about ministry without a deeper understanding of the ways in which the minister can make his own wounds available as a source of healing.*[1]

It was out of Brenda's own woundedness and subsequent healing that she found the desire to help others, going back to school and getting her counseling degree in midlife.

"May I read something you wrote about when you first began experiencing grace?"

Brenda nodded and slipped me some yellowed sheets of paper, looking on with a combination of hope and concern.

> *It was mid-April, and spring was making a slow start in Texas. Shades of green stippled the landscape, announcing growth and life to come. Today, the signs of life along the creekside stood in stark contrast to the cold deadness of my*

soul. I dragged my old wooden rocking chair out onto the back deck to sit in the morning sun. Still cold, I wrapped myself in an old afghan my mother had crocheted. Rocking back and forth, clutching a little red children's book tightly to my chest, I heard the old wooden rocker creaking and groaning as if to complain under the strain of my weight.

Perhaps I had come to the trees for an embrace I had once wanted from my mother when I was small and feeling lonely. How I had longed to be held and sung to, but Mother was usually busy. Today, the finches were flitting from tree to tree, singing as they busily gathered twigs and seeds. Here I sat, alone, in the lap of nature.

Flipping through the pages of the little red storybook I'd treasured since childhood, I came to some old favorites. "The Crooked Family." "Five Peas in a Pod." "The Lost Lamb." I smiled for the first time in days as I noticed little smudges of sticky stuff, perhaps tiny chips of a childhood lollipop. And little splashes of hot chocolate. I rubbed my hand over the pages, as if trying to reconnect with something familiar. It was that same little-girl loneliness coming over me again. Longing for God's embrace, to have some sign that He cared.

"God, You say You love me. I don't feel loved," I declared out loud. If His grace was not true for me, I was ready to know it and stop pretending. "Are you really a good God?" I asked. "I want to believe You love me, but the truth is, my sins are more real to me than You are."

As I let my mind carry me back to earlier days, the failures of my past flashed before me as they had so many times before . . .

In my angry, self-condemning state I weakly called out to God. Clearly, He hadn't responded to tireless spiritual pursuit. Maybe my honest, though angry, heart was more inviting than my usual efforts to impress Him. The truth is, I don't know why God decided to bless me with His presence that day, any more than I understand why He hadn't done it the day before, or the day before that, or the day before that.

It was mid-afternoon when I began to sense His presence, a warmth more intense than the sun's rays. There was no audible voice from heaven, and He did not visibly appear. I just knew He was there. Like a balm of concentrated forgiveness being massaged directly into my heart, I began to feel comforted, held, blessed.

I closed my eyes, trying to picture how Jesus might look with "skin on." In my mind's eye, Jesus stood before me, and I was aware that I didn't want to look into His face. But the warmth of His presence quickly overcame my impulse to revisit. For the first time I could recall, I was looking into the face of Jesus. To my amazement, He was smiling. And I realized I hadn't expected Him to smile. Perhaps I thought He'd peer down His nose at me through lenses of legalism, judging my past mistakes as harshly as I judged myself. Instead, He was gazing into my eyes with tenderness and compassion such as I'd never seen or felt.

Still rocking, I basked in His loving presence. After a few minutes, thoughts began to come. Jesus loves me. Reaching for a spiral notebook and pen, I wrote down: Jesus loves me. The reality of the words on the page began to sink into my heart, as I gratefully returned His gaze. More thoughts came into my mind, and then flowed from pen to paper:

"I was a lonely little girl . . . and Jesus loved me.

"I tried to make my first marriage work, but I could not . . . and Jesus loved me.

"My children suffered pain and loss due, in part, to my actions . . . and Jesus loved me.

"I got angry at God because I didn't get the answers I wanted . . . and Jesus loved me.

"I threw up my hands and admitted failure . . . and Jesus loved me.

"There is hope for my future . . . because Jesus loves me."[2]

When I looked up from reading, there was a moment of gentle, holy silence—even the sound of our breathing seemed like prayer. The Holy Spirit was in this humble kitchen, as sure as the sunlight pouring on the warm wooden table in front of us.

"You have a gift, Brenda," I finally said. "You need to share this."

Brenda's eyes crinkled at the corners as an enormous smile spread across her face. Apparently, I'd touched what I call a "heartstone"—a soul gift waiting for the appointed time of its release, much as a racehorse stands ready to explode in a run as soon as the starting gate is lifted.

"You like it? Really?" Brenda asked incredulously. "You think I could do this? I've dreamed about writing for so long, but I don't know where to begin. I know how busy you are, so I hate to ask. But would you consider giving me writing lessons?"

"I have to admit," I said thoughtfully, "my plate is awfully full right now. I can't add anything else to it unless it is obviously from God—but I have a feeling this might be one of those things. And Brenda, if a little of who you are rubs off on me, that will be payment enough. How about I help you get started writing professionally, and you help me grow in the kind of grace you write about here?"

And so, the gate lifted and we were off with a gallop. Almost weekly we began meeting for pancakes at IHOP or chicken salad at Applebee's or yogurt at TCBY. Our faces became so familiar to the waitresses, they began asking us if we just wanted "our regular selections" from the menu—and automatically brought coffee halfway through our meals, the way we liked it. Once, a waitress saw me coming in from the parking lot and opened the door saying, "She's up in the corner booth waiting for you. Have fun!"

Often Brenda and I would celebrate the occasion—any occasion would do—with cards or small gifts. Most often those gifts and cards were "little girlish" in nature. One card I cherish is a watercolor of an adorable young girl braiding her friend's hair. Inside the card Brenda wrote, "This is what you are to me. You are my dear friend and editor, 'braiding up' my writing—helping it read prettier."

When my book, *A View from the Porch Swing*, debuted, Brenda ordered me a special Kim Anderson figurine of a little girl on a tree swing. She has an adorable face, framed by a straw hat, and is delicately painted in hues of taupe and soft pink with a music box base that plays "Beautiful Dreamer."

And that's what we are when we are together—beautiful dreamers. Dreamers of stories and books and ideas. Dreamers of places we want to go and explore someday—oceans and mountains and quaint little villages, along with spiritual destinations of joy and freedom.

As Brenda's writing began to take shape, I could see her message was about vulnerability, opening up, and becoming more real with ourselves, with God, and with others. I could sense a book was about to be birthed in her, and I felt privileged to stand by as a sort of midwife. One morning I awoke with a book title playing about my mind. *It's for Brenda's book!* I realized. Just then the phone rang and, still groggy from sleep, I let the answering machine pick it up. "Good morning, Becky!" sang the familiar voice of my friend.

I picked up the receiver and echoed, "Good morning, Brenda!" but before she could say why she'd called I said, "I woke up with a thought for your book. An idea for a title. You are writing about being 'real,' right? And you have such love for children's books: we've often talked about how your life parallels *The Velveteen Rabbit*. How about calling your book *The Velveteen Woman?*"

There was a short moment of silence and then I heard Brenda's childlike squeal of delight followed by, "Becky! I love it!"

And so we worked on her proposal and sent it to editors. That done, we began the hard part: we held our breath and prayed. One bright morning we gathered at IHOP to breakfast and do what writers love most—*talk* about writing. (I know several dozen authors, and all of them prefer *talking* about writing over actually *writing*.)

After the waitress took our order, Brenda handed me a gift-wrapped box and said, "I want you to have this now, before we find out whether the book will be accepted or rejected by a publisher. Because either way, I want you to know this whole experience has been a gift. I've never had so much fun."

I reached into the box and pulled out the cuddliest, floppiest, softest stuffed bunny rabbit a grown-up little girl could ever want. On instinct, I gave the fluffy toy a welcoming hug. At that moment, my husband, Scott, walked into the restaurant and over to our booth. He'd just come from the doctor's office and, knowing I was here, wanted to deliver good news about the results of a medical test—one we'd both been worried about.

"Looks like I'm gonna live to aggravate you a few more years," he said with a grin. Then looking down at us, he added, "Cute bunny." Scott reached for the stuffed rabbit, held it tightly in his arms, and sat down beside me in the booth with visible relief. A few minutes later, our mutual friend, Gracie Malone, also happened by. Before long, we were having an impromptu pancake party of praise.

After breakfast Scott and I walked out to the parking lot together, saying our good-byes to Gracie Malone and Brenda Waggoner as we went. Just before we each headed for our respective cars, Brenda ran back toward us, holding a cell phone to her ear, a smile breaking over her face. "Hold on, you guys!" she shouted. "You've got to listen to this. It must have been left on my recorder while we were eating breakfast."

The three of us put our heads together and Brenda replayed the message into our assembled ears. We could hear the enthusiastic voice of an editor saying, "Brenda, I wanted to call you personally with some great news. We presented several proposals at our board meeting today, and yours was the hit of the show. There was excitement all around, and the vote was unanimous: we would like to offer you a contract for *The Velveteen Woman*."

Even today, nearly a year later, Scott and Brenda and I can recall those moments of pure, unadulterated joy as we each experienced that sun-kissed morning—that day of bright, blessed good news. Just last week, Brenda went to a convention for therapists, and when she was asked to describe one moment where she felt completely, joyfully affirmed, she chose this very moment as the moment to share.

Encouraged by the momentum of a real book offer, Brenda began to write in earnest. As icing on the contract, the publisher hired me as outside editor for the project. As chapter on chapter unfolded, the bargain we struck that rainy day in Brenda's kitchen poured down blessings on both our heads.

Brenda was growing so fast as a writer, I began to feel as Anne Sullivan must have felt about Helen Keller at some point in time: the student was growing beyond the teacher. Brenda's stories also opened my eyes to the realms of joy I longed to experience in my own life.

A few weeks ago, at our traditional writing/lunch meeting, Brenda walked over to our table and handed me one perfect white rose, wrapped in tissue and ribbon. A gift, just because she loved me as a friend. No matter how much I insisted that she was a writer in her own right now, she constantly expressed her gratitude for my being her "teacher."

"I've had many friends over the years," I said, as I fingered the soft petals of the rose, feeling especially vulnerable and grateful to be so treasured. "I believe I've loved all of them. But none has been as good for me as you have been. I not only love you, I love the person you are helping me to become. I am happier in my relationship with God, with my husband and kids, with people in general and with my life than I've ever been. So much of that is not because of what you've 'taught' me, but because of what I've 'caught' by just being around you. You've represented God's grace to me, Brenda, in a way I don't think I could have seen otherwise."

With typical Brenda-like openness, she leaned forward and said, "I think that's the nicest thing anybody could ever say about me. Thank you for having eyes to see the good things God's put in me."

I understand now, as perhaps never before, the kind of love that existed between King David and his beloved friend Jonathan. Brenda and I are not only writing buddies and lunchmates, we are something much deeper than that: we are truly Anne-of-Green-Gable-esque "kindred spirits and bosom buddies."

And on some inexplicable emotional level, we are two little girls on a porch swing, talking and giggling and swinging our legs to the rhythm and wonder of grace.

On Accepting Grace

"I say to you, unless you are converted and become as little children, you will by no means enter the kingdom of heaven. Therefore whoever humbles himself as this little child is the greatest in the kingdom of heaven."

—*Matthew 18:3–4 NKJV*

"Jesus cuts to the heart of the matter as he sits the child on his knee. The child is unself-conscious, incapable of pretense . . .

"The child doesn't have to struggle to get himself in a good position for having a relationship with God; he doesn't have to craft ingenious ways of explaining his position to Jesus; he doesn't have to create a pretty face for himself; he doesn't have to achieve any state of spiritual feeling or intellectual understanding. All he has to do is happily accept the cookies: the gift of the kingdom."[3]

—*Brennan Manning, The Ragamuffin Gospel*

"A saint is not someone who is good but someone who experiences the goodness of God."[4]

—*Thomas Merton*

Volunteer!
You can learn it later!
—Suzie Humphreys

Whirlybird Wildflower

I took a deep breath and dialed the phone. John Wayne answered.

Or at least that's what Suzie Humphreys calls her husband, a long tall Texan who goes by the name of Tom.

"Hey, Tom," I said, "this is Becky Freeman. I'm the writer who's driving down from Greenville to visit your charming wife tomorrow. If I'm not mistaken, she invited me to spend the night in, was it, your *airplane hangar*?"

"That's right. We've made a little guest room next to the hangar where I restore old war planes. You're gonna love Fredericksburg too. Most women think they're in heaven when they see all the shops. At least that's what Suzie thought when we moved here from Dallas a few years back."

"Well, I'm a certified shopper so I'll allow time to make the rounds downtown. And I can't wait to see your ranch. I've heard it's something special."

Tom was open and friendly as we chatted about our work, our common East Texas background, and how I came to admire his wife and her gifts of communication.

"I heard Suzie give an amazing speech at a time in my life when I was terrified to address an audience," I explained. "Funny thing, Tom—but did you know people think just because you can write a book, you can also speak in coherent sentences in front of big crowds?"

"Nah . . ."

"Yes! And I'm here to tell you, the two don't necessarily go hand in hand. So I went to this meeting of the National Speaker's Association hoping to get some pointers—before I trusted myself with a microphone on stage—and that's when I heard Suzie's keynote, the one called 'I Can Do That!'"

"That's a good one," Tom commented.

"It was incredible! Not like a canned speech—just Suzie being Suzie. Funny, passionate, in-your-face honest. I can't tell you if I cried more from the tender truths she shared, or from laughing so hard at her funny stories, but I left that meeting forever changed. Her enthusiasm was infectious—exactly the encouragement I needed at a vulnerable time. Is she always that way? I mean at home and all?"

"Here's God's honest truth," Tom said with emphasis. "I've been married to Suzie for twenty-three years and I think she's the most optimistic woman who ever drew breath."

"*That's* what I want to talk to her about. I want to find out where she got her upbeat attitude. Do you know how rare that is? I mean how does a person acquire that 'ain't life grand' outlook?"

"Well," Tom drawled, "you'll just have to come out to the ranch and find out. Be sure and ask Suzie about her mother. She inherited lots of spunk from her. You got a pencil?"

"Yep," I answered.

"Then here's the directions . . ."

A few minutes later, after hanging up the phone, I thought, *I can't believe I'm going to get to visit with Suzie Humphreys. And spend the night in an airplane hangar to boot!*

From Suzie's speech at the NSA event, I remembered that

she and Tom had been Dallas dwellers for years—though Tom had always been a country guy at heart. He'd grown particularly enamored with a lovely parcel of southwest Texas known as "the hill country." He and Suzie had even dreamed of moving there, but Big D was synonymous with home, friends, job security, and local celebrityhood. You'd be hard pressed to find a Dallasite that doesn't recognize the name Suzie Humphreys.

Suzie's media career began when she became one of the most popular television hosts ever to grace the metroplex with her hilarity and down-to-earth style. As hostess for "News 8, Etc." she interviewed several U.S. presidents, shot rifles with John Wayne (the real one), played poker with Omar Sharif, received red roses on her birthday from Gene Hackman, laughed with Carol Burnett, cooked dinner at her apartment for Clint Eastwood . . .

Her next long-term job was hosting the morning show with popular personality, Ron Chapman, on top-rated KVIL radio station. Most people, actually, know Suzie as "that hilarious lady who rode around in a helicopter talking on the radio to Ron Chapman." Suzie had come a long way from her beginnings as a little red-headed, blue-eyed gal who once lived in Hereford, Texas, a small town in the Texas panhandle. With practically no college, no resumé, and no experience, Suzie had made it into the big time on sheer optimism, hard work, resilience—and a lot of help from God. Then one day Suzie looked at Tom and said, "I've had a wonderful time here, but, Tom, it's your turn. You go find your rainbow."

Within a few months, Tom found an old cabin in Fredericksburg, on the acreage of his dreams at a price they could afford, and he and Suzie and their son Josh (now twenty-one) proceeded to relocate their lives, country-style.

I, for one, couldn't wait to see the results with my own eyes.

So I loaded up Big Red (my faithful Chevy van) and headed south. The seven hours passed quickly as I absorbed the beautiful rolling hills and quaint scenery. For a stretch of several miles, I passed dozens of peach orchards. I thought about peaches until I could hold out no longer. I was finally done in by a hand painted sign—"Fresh Homemade Peach Ice Cream." As if by magnetic pull, my van parked itself in front of the fruit stand, which was run by a family with lots of happy, barefoot children. I walked in for a quick look-see, and came out with a Styrofoam cup full of calories. As I licked the last bite of frozen peach sweetness from the plastic spoon, I decided my indulgence had been worth the sin.

Once on the road again, I resisted the urge to turn off at the sign for Luckenbach, Texas, where Waylon and Willie and the Boys are known to gather to sing country songs and drink long-necks until "there ain't nobody feeling no pain." (I don't think Waylon and Willie and the Boys do this year-round, mind you. However, I hear they have quite the pain-free shindig in Luckenbach every Fourth of July.)

Soon, I arrived at Fredericksburg's main street (Tom was right, the town square is enough to raise the blood pressure of any shopping woman), turned right on Tivydale Road—going up Tivys and down Dales for several more miles—until, finally, I turned into the gated ranch and drove up a gravel road to a cottage charming enough to belong to a family of porridge-eating bears.

So this is the end of Tom's rainbow, I thought with a smile.

And there, in all her red-headed, wide-smiled glory, stood Suzie Humphreys on the front porch.

"Are you Becky?" she shouted.

"I'm afraid I am," I said as I walked toward the cabin.

"How are you doin'?" Suzie's voice was as friendly as her eager smile.

The cabin seemed so tiny on the outside that I'd wondered if it could truly be "the main house," but once inside I was surprised by its roomy feel and commented on it.

"It's the original cabin, but with the tall ceilings it still gives the place an open feeling," Suzie explained. "Come get the big two-room tour!"

Suzie's home was, as she said, just two main, big rooms—but oh, those two rooms! Lots of stained and painted wood, splashed with decorative touches of forest greens, burnt sienna, navy blues, sun-splashed yellows, and dark reds. A virtual artist's palette of Mexican pottery, serapes, stripes, checks, lace, and love—lots of love.

"We're taking you to dinner at The Oak House," Suzie remarked matter-of-factly. "Tom will follow in his truck so you and I can get acquainted on the way there."

"Sounds perfect, I'm starved!"

Once buckled in the car, Suzie wasted no time in asking how she could help me.

"There's a thousand questions I could ask," I said, "but mostly, I want to know how you came to have such an optimistic outlook on life. Tom said to ask about your mother."

"Oh, yes. My mother is eighty-eight years old, housebound, in pain most of the time—and she's one of the happiest, most well-adjusted people I know. She never feels sorry for herself. No time to. She's too interested in life."

"Was she always like this?"

"From the time I was a little girl, my mother had to work to make ends meet. And every blessed day when she woke up, no matter how cold or how early, she would swing her legs over the side of the bed and say, 'I get to go to work today!'"

I wondered what would happen if we all started our mornings with such a confession of joy. "Suzie, I'd love to know more about what you've learned to help you navigate life's storms with good humor."

"Well, I'm twenty years older than you, Becky, and I can tell you I've had lots of learning to do. I've always been optimistic, but I was so self-absorbed until Josh was born. I had no idea what it meant to really put another human being ahead of myself. I think one of the big keys to life is to survive until you get it together."

"And how old were you when Josh was born?"

"I was forty. When I was pregnant I was nauseated every day. And flying in that helicopter! I'd check the traffic and throw up, get on the air, then throw up some more."

"I want to hear how you got that job, by the way."

"I'll let you listen to some of my tapes if you like—most of my stories are on them."

"I can't wait."

We arrived at the restaurant and Tom sauntered up to meet us. He was tall and handsome, a man's man, a Texan—what can I say? He was *John Wayne*. Dinner proved one of the best I've ever eaten, but what struck me most about the evening was the parade of friends dropping by to say hello and chat. From the cook to the restaurant owner and his wife, to the mayor of Luckenbach—after awhile I simply lost count. And no person seemed an interruption.

Not to Tom and Suzie.

Every person was unique, every one with a story worth hearing. For example, the owner had recently cut his trademark ponytail. Most people would remark about it in passing.

Not to Tom and Suzie.

Questions poured out of them both, like twin inquisitors. "Now tell us, what does cutting your hair really symbolize to you? What new stage of life are you entering?" A remarkable discussion ensued. Tom and Suzie are experts at inviting others to open up. *Restaurant therapists*, I thought with a grin.

Before we finished dinner yet another set of their friends stopped by the table and asked us to please, please drop by their home for a quick visit. "Of course!" was the ready answer. *I've landed in the friendliest town in America,* I thought.

I asked Suzie, as she drove us home late that night, how she'd befriended so many of the Fredericksburg natives. Most of them were probably unaware of Suzie's Dallas celebrity status—she was just plain Suzie to her friends here. And she loved that. Being a "big name" had long lost its importance to her. Being all that God wants her to be, at whatever cost, living life to its fullest, loving people—these have long since taken the place of celebrity's glitter.

"You asked about friends and that reminds me of something I wanted to tell you. I can't abide it when people whine, 'I never get out. No one ever asks me over.' When we moved here, Tom and I didn't wait for invitations or neighbors to come calling. We immediately announced a neighborhood garage sale, sent invitations to the entire neighborhood asking them to join us and we hosted a preview party. Everyone stayed and stayed—many of the neighbors hadn't even met each other before."

"What a fabulous idea."

"Oh, and some of us have started a group called COW."

What else could I expect from a lady who lived in Hereford?

"Dare I ask what COW stands for?" I asked.

"Company of Women. We meet for no purpose whatsoever."

She drove up to the little guest room in the hangar and I was thrilled to see it decorated with as much attention and love as her own cottage home. Battenburg lace, quilts, a red-and-white striped overstuffed love seat, charming touches of plaid and checks, needlepoint pillows (I couldn't help smiling at the one that said, "Clint Eastwood sat here"), a refrigerator stocked with goodies, interesting movies, and books. Personal touches were everywhere: framed quotes and verses, precious photos of Tom teasing and laughing with a young Josh. As restful as it was, I had brain energy to burn so I snuggled up in the antique twin bed and popped in one of Suzie's taped cassettes, my heart warming to her down-home stories.

In her message called "Life is What Happens to You While You're Making Other Plans," Suzie shared how, after she'd spent all her "celebrity" money on a fancy car and alligator shoes, she was fired—CANNED!—from her morning TV show. She soon found herself broke and depressed with a capital D—in Big D. Worse yet, no one would hire her because they were afraid their jobs wouldn't be exciting enough for her. ("Yeah," she chuckled sarcastically, "like food stamps would have been excitin'. . .")

I laughed out loud at the philosophy about depression Suzie worked out during those dark days of unemployment.

"I believe if you are depressed you should—give in to it! Oh, they don't tell you that at the psychiatrist, do they? They tell you to go be with people. But when you are depressed, who do you think wants to be with you? You go be with people when you're depressed, you won't have a friend left. No, that's not what you do.

"First thing you got to do is admit you're depressed. 'I am depressed!' There's no sin in it, say it! Pick up the phone and call into the office and tell 'em you're not coming in today—you are depressed.

"Now, go into your room and close the door. Put on that ol' robe you have—you know that robe, the one with the grape stains on it. Next—now this is real important—do NOT wash your hair. You know how good you look with oily hair. You women, don't wear that waterproof mascara; wear that kind that beads down the side of your face in big smudges. Now go take a look at yourself in the bathroom mirror. You're so ugly, you get more depressed. Now that's good! That's what you want!

"Then get into bed, pull the covers up and start crying— and don't be Minnie Mouse about it either. CRY. Wail. Moan and agonize. You need help thinking of sad things? Death will get you on a roll every time. Lie there and think of someone you loved who dumped you. (Well?! You been crying over that one for—what?—seven or eight years?)

Lie there. Think of everything sad you can think of: the world situation, how awful everything is . . . And cry some more. Let it come from your toes all the way up to the top of your head.

"If you really give in to your depression, in two hours— maximum time—you will so-o-o-ob your last tear and think, God, I'm sick of this.

"Then you get up and go get some Mexican food.

"See, it's so simple . . ."[1]

As I was still giggling over Suzie's cure for depression, she launched into the story of how she again found a job "out of the blue." A call came in from Ron Chapman.

"Suzie," Ron said, "our reporter in the helicopter is going on vacation, and we thought it might be interesting for you to do the traffic reports."

"A traffic reporter? In a helicopter?" Suzie asked. "How much does it pay?"

Ron told her the amount, and without missing a beat Suzie replied, "Yes, I can be a traffic reporter in a helicopter." (Here it should be mentioned that a famous Suzie motto is, "Volunteer! You can learn it later!")

So at six o'clock Monday morning, Suzie drove down to meet the helicopter pilot and get a crash course (pardon the pun) in traffic reporting. "Now listen," Suzie tells her audiences, "I hadn't thought that much about what a traffic reporter does. First of all, a traffic reporter has to know *where he is.* How many of you women really have the need to use the words *north, south, east,* or *west* in your vocabulary? When someone asks you where the grocery store is, doesn't 'left' work for *you*?"

There was precious little time to get oriented before the helicopter took off. Once airborne, Suzie faced a confusing array of buttons. When, after forty-five slow minutes she finally spotted an accident, she became so excited she pushed the wrong button. ("A funny thing happens to you when you are a traffic reporter," she confessed. "You get sick in the head. You pray for a wreck, so you'll have something to report.")

Instead of talking to the radio host, Ron Chapman, Suzie ended up broadcasting her discovery to the entire metroplex.

"I FOUND ONE!" she yelled with excitement. Her announcement came right in the middle of a song by Engelbert Humperdink. Err, err, err, went the record as Ron Chapman, ever smooth, came on the air and said, "Yes, Suzie Humphreys in the 'KVIL-icopter' found one *what*?"

"A WRECK!!"

"No, no, no," said Ron, "We don't refer to them as wrecks at this radio station. We say 'accident.'"

"Well, this one's a WRECK!"

"All right, then where is it?"

"Well it's across from a brick house and down the street from a Texaco station," she answered matter-of-factly.

"Suzie," Ron said, "We need you to be more specific."

"Listen, Ron, if you're in it, you know where it is. And if you're not, you don't care."

And so it went. From bad to worse. The show was so bad, so horribly bad in fact that it was a huge hit. People called in all day asking, "Is she for REAL?" or pleading, "Oh, have her back on again." Suzie said, "All over Dallas-Fort Worth men were sitting in their cars that fateful morning thinking, 'My gosh! That's my WIFE up there!'"

Within two weeks, Suzie found herself once again, delightfully, unusually, and gainfully employed as the permanent traffic reporter.

I turned off the tape and chuckled myself to sleep.

The next morning, I woke up refreshed, walked out to a little patio next to the guest room, sat down in a lawn chair and wrote in my journal:

I can't believe I am here—wrapped in a soft flannel robe, cocooned by the morning breeze, serenaded by chirping birds and the deep low of a cow, looking out over the Texas hills. Oh, what a beautiful morning, Lord, please give us a beautiful day.

After a shower and change, I met Suzie for a leisurely breakfast at The Peach Tree restaurant, intending to say good-bye there. But when she asked if I'd like to go with her to her nail appointment, I was delighted.

Suzie's friend and "nail lady" operated out of her home, which was painted, in its entirety, a blazing color of hot purple-pink. As always, Suzie introduced me, making me feel as special as possible. "This is Becky Freeman. She writes BOOKS. Just up and WRITES them!"

At the manicurist's instructions, Suzie dipped her hands into hot melted wax, winced a bit—the price of beauty—and asked if I had any more questions.

"I do have one more," I said, resting my head on my hand. "If you could describe your idea of a perfect day, what would it be like?"

Without hesitation Suzie answered, "I'd get up in the morning and see a mountain and a river—first thing. One of our favorite places in all the world is Creed, Colorado. We have so many good family memories there. I wouldn't have a plan at all. I'd read a good book. And I'd cook something! I get excited about cooking when I have time to enjoy it. Yes, I'd put on a pot of something and cook it real slow. We might go out to see a good movie and sometime during the day, I'd go out to a favorite spot—maybe a mountain lake, and just be grateful."

Here, tears formed on Suzie's eyelids and spilled over. She enunciated her words carefully, slowly, her voice full of emotion. "I am just so grateful to *feel.* We have such a short time here. Why do we wait to enjoy it?"

Why, indeed? I thought. And I realized this attitude of thankfulness is the secret of an enthusiastic, optimistic heart.

Later that morning as we parted company, Suzie admonished me to go shopping downtown and have a ball. "Eat the good local food," she said, "and don't feel the least bit guilty." I must admit, I stopped at a pay phone to check on my kids and husband, but once assured the house would not burn down without me, I drank up every drop of Suzie's advice.

I shopped 'til I dropped. Had an absolute ball. Didn't feel a shred of guilt. Headed for home renewed, refreshed, and ready to write all I had gleaned from this remarkable lady.

As I drove home, I spied the peach stand again—the one with the homemade ice cream and barefooted kids—and almost passed it by. But I thought better of it and turned in at the last minute. Like ice cream, life is short-lived and sweet.

While we are here, why not savor every bit of goodness God grants us?

On Optimism

(Inspiration from Suzie Humphreys' Guest House Walls)

The Doer

"It is not the critic who counts; not the man who points out how the strong man stumbled or where the doer of deeds could have done better.

"The credit belongs to the man who is actually in the arena, whose face is marred by dust and sweat and blood, who strives valiantly; who tries and comes short again and again . . .

"Who spends himself in a worthy cause, who knows the triumph of great achievement; and who, at worst, if he fails, at least fails while daring greatly, so that his place shall never be with those cold and timid souls who knew neither victory or defeat."

—*Theodore Roosevelt*

"Youth is not entirely a time of life as it is a state of mind. It is not wholly a matter of ripe cheeks, red lips, and supple knees. It is a temper of will, a quality of the imagination, a vigor of the emotions."

—*Source Unknown*

"With all its sham, drudgery, and broken dreams, it is still a beautiful world."

—*Desiderata found on Old St. Paul's Cathedral, Baltimore*

A child was dying . . .
How could I say no?
—Melissa Gantt

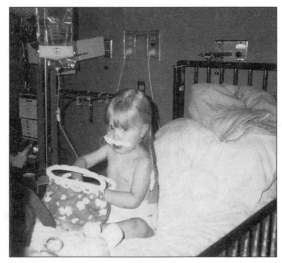

Lynsey in 1991

Melissa and Lynsey

A Gift of Flowering Hope

My friend and neighbor, Melissa Gantt, is Ethel to my Lucy (or sometimes Lucy to my Ethel) and my traveling companion in this sometimes times painful, ofttimes hilarious, journey of life.

First, down the path of hilarity.

A couple of years ago, Melissa and I took an unforgettable minivacation to Hollywood, California, together. (Not surprisingly, we lingered nearly two hours in the *I Love Lucy* memorabilia at Universal Studios.)

Several scenes flash through my mind even now and bring a smile to my lips. An interesting ride down an escalator in an airport is one of them.

Both us were neck deep in luggage. I do not know what possessed Melissa to do this, but she insisted I go ahead of her. When I reached the bottom of the escalator, I managed to step off with some measure of grace. However, my suitcase was much heavier than I realized and I discovered too late—and to our mutual shock—that I did not have the strength to drag it off with me. There it sat, like an ominous road block, stuck on the bottom step. Which meant that Melissa had to finish her descent—both arms wrapped around luggage—by straddling my oversized suitcase and letting it pass between her legs. The only other alternative would have been to trip and fall face forward on the floor. To complete this cartoon-like scenario, I might add, Melissa was wearing a dress.

Even as I type this, I am laughing again, recalling Melissa's quick thinking, albeit unladylike, maneuver.

Yet another *I Love Lucy* episode occurred upon boarding the plane to go home. We'd purchased a dozen huge cinnamon rolls for our children, each one the size of a full-grown cantaloupe, and placed them in a paper shopping bag—to add to our mounting bulk of baggage. Much to our amazement, as we stepped onto the airplane, the bag broke loose, releasing the rolls. They looked like a dozen gummy bowling balls gone wild as they veered crazily down the alley and under passenger seats.

"Catch that big one coming toward you!" one flight attendant called out to another, in a futile effort to stem the "roll-ing" tide. As one stewardess directed people to pass our wayward sticky buns to the front of the aircraft, I couldn't help thinking, *When the rolls are called up yonder, I'll be there.*

It appears to me, the friends we hold most dear are those who've survived some sort of a crisis or two with us—or in the very least, with whom we've shared some hearty laughter. Melissa and I have done both, and often, both at once.

Unfortunately, this past year held fewer laughs and more pain for my friend. Last summer Melissa survived a major back surgery, resulting in her having to wear a body cast for three months. She pulled through it like a trooper, but little did she know this would be the beginning of "The Year from Hell."

Soon after this surgery, extended family relationships went through a tumultuous period. Anybody with family and parents and in-laws and misunderstandings, who lives long enough, usually passes through a similar experience; the resulting pain and confusion of valued relationships gone awry—even temporarily—can often defy explanation.

Just as Melissa began to feel she was getting back on her feet, physically and emotionally, she took a fall (off an eight-inch step!) that so badly broke and twisted her leg that her foot was turned nearly backwards. Immediately, she was ushered into emergency surgery. She awoke to the physician's orders: she would have to confine herself to a cast and crutches for three months. Another long-anticipated summer put on hold for repairs.

Have you ever had a time in your life when you felt the world was raining down so hard and so fast it almost hurt to wake up in the morning? In times like these we tend to forget the light in our lives, the joy we were born to give, the great things God once worked in and through us and will work again. At the core of whirling pain, we are desperate to latch on to who we are, and why we are here—to anything that feels like hope.

It was at a time such as this in Melissa's life that we chose to go see the movie *Hope Floats*. Thankfully, we'd stopped to purchase two packs of Kleenex beforehand. Melissa hobbled through the theater on crutches and cast, while I followed behind with purses and popcorn in tow. (This time, Melissa remembered the wisdom of walking in FRONT of me rather than behind me.)

During several of the movie's more poignant scenes, I dabbed at my eyes—but when I looked to my left, Melissa was nearly convulsed in tears. So quickly was she soaking tissues, I offered her the last half of my packet, whispering, "You just let it all out. You've earned a good cry." She smiled weakly, blew her nose, and reached for another tissue.

I mulled over the two-word title of the film for several days, appreciating more and more the life-affirming message it sent. For even when human beings, and our own bodies, fail us, God's gift of hope is ever resilient, finding its way to the surface of life's pain-filled ponds.

And so it happened one golden afternoon, not long after our "chick flick" outing, Melissa asked me to come over for a visit.

When I arrived, classical music was pouring from the stereo. She invited me out to the back porch where we sat looking over the lake where we live, the lake where we raise our kids as if they are almost one big family, sharing boat rides and fishing spots and cups of sugar, along with hugs and orders (to "Clean up that mess!") and late-night conversations.

Melissa lowered herself carefully into a lawn chair and laughed. "Becky," she said as she chuckled, "I found your Gabe sitting in my kitchen the other day. He had a bar stool pulled up to the pantry and was looking through it with the most discouraged look on his face, since he couldn't find a thing worth snacking on. When he saw me come in, he looked up nonchalantly and asked when I was going to fix supper."

Indeed Gabe refers to the Gantts as his second family. Melissa's daughter, Sarah, is much like a sister to Gabe, and Melissa's son, Josh, is as close to Gabe as his own brothers. For a few months of the summer my Rachel and Melissa's Josh had a bit of a romance going, and in spite of ourselves—and our determination not to become involved—Melissa and I couldn't help wondering if someday we might become in-laws.

"If we do," I said, "I want us to promise each other one thing."

"What's that?" Melissa asked.

"No matter what our kids do—we stay friends."

"It's a deal," she quickly agreed.

As we munched on Melissa's homemade cranberry scones and sipped at iced mocha lattes, I leaned back in my chair, inhaling the beauty of the moment. The soothing music, the rippling lake, the delicious treats spoke a silent truth: Hope was bubbling up once again in this home.

"Melissa, how are you doing?" I asked. "I mean how are you *really* doing?"

"Better," she replied thoughtfully. "I still really need to be around people who see the best in me. I'm stronger, but still fragile. Does that make sense?"

"Having been there myself, I do understand. But just for the record, I think you are an incredible person."

Sure, Melissa's house usually looks like a bomb hit it. So does mine, so this only serves to endear her to me. And sure, she's forgetful sometimes, loses things, has strong opinions, and has—or perhaps I should say, *had*—a desire to right all wrongs in the world. After some quality time in counselors' chairs, both of us are realizing the futility of fixer-hood.

However, Melissa's desire to help the underdog remains strong, and is a part of who she will always be. And if you happen to be low dog on the canine pole, this trait is a godsend.

In fact, there's also something Christlike about the championing of underdogs. God was always cheering on some lost cause, casting His vote for least likely candidates—from a little shepherd boy facing a giant with a sling full of stones; to Israel, the smallest of nations; His radical plan to save the world, starting with a babe in a manger.

I put my legs up on the deck railing to catch the sun's rays. (Our motto is, "Tanned fat looks better than white fat.") My thoughts turned to a specific incident of Melissa's benevolence, one I wanted to hear more about. "Melissa, would you tell me about you and Lynsey?"

I'd heard from Michael, Melissa's husband, that there was quite a story to be told about Melissa and a little girl, a desperately sick child named Lynsey.

"Well," began Melissa, "for a long time I didn't want to tell this to many people, but I think it may be time to do it. I didn't want to draw attention to myself, but I'm realizing there may be a greater good that can come from sharing it." She shifted comfortably in her chair, took a sip of her latte, and dove into the tale.

"When Michael and I lived in Austin, we lived next door to a young couple named Becky and Ed. Their son, Jordan, and my Josh became fast friends. They were almost inseparable." Melissa went on to explain that after many years of waiting and praying, God granted Ed and Becky a second child, a little girl, whom they named Lynsey.

"Becky's a schoolteacher—and you know how they tend to be extra observant. When Lynsey was about thirteen months old, Becky noticed her daughter's eyes looked awfully puffy. The next day Becky took Lynsey to the pediatrician, expecting to be told she was an overcautious mom. But after what seemed like hours, the doctor returned with the report. 'For some unknown reason,' he said, 'Lynsey appears to be spilling protein into her urine.'

"The next day, they sent Lynsey for some medical tests and eventually discovered she had Nephrotic Syndrome caused by a rare disease: Focal Segmental Gomerlular Schrosis. Sadly, we got lots of practice pronouncing this illness, because short of a kidney transplant—there is no cure.

"The doctors assured Ed and Becky this was a slow-moving disease. Through medication, Lindsey might be able to keep her own kidneys for up to five years.

"Then, just nine months later, a biopsy showed the disease had spread much more rapidly than any of them had expected. Lynsey's kidneys were functioning at fifteen percent of a normal organ."

Melissa sighed and shook her head, sadly recalling how fast Lynsey went downhill, and how desperate her dear friends began to feel. "Lynsey dropped off the bottom of the growth chart. By the time she turned two her entire body was puffed up, filled with toxins her kidneys could no longer filter. The doctors said it was time to consider a transplant. Of course Ed and Becky were tested, but for medical reasons they were unable to be donors."

"Melissa, how could a tiny child like Lynsey receive an adult-sized kidney anyway?" I asked, curious.

"You know, that's really interesting. An adult can donate a kidney to a child, and the kidney will actually shrink to fit. The donor's remaining kidney will also swell to accommodate the lost organ."

"I had no idea. The human body is so amazing," I mused. "So what happened next?"

"About that time, our family moved from Austin to Houston. We stayed in close contact with Ed and Becky, however. When Becky called one day she told me Lynsey's blood type was O negative. I drew in a breath and held it. After I hung up, I told Michael and the kids I wanted to be tested as a possible donor for Lynsey."

"How did they react?"

"There was some concern among family and friends, even some outright protest, but Michael and I were in agreement. All we had to do was glance at our two healthy kids and know how we'd feel if one of them were in Lynsey's condition. This child was dying and I had an opportunity to possibly help her live, with minimal risk to my long-term health. How could I say no?"

"Melissa, lots of people would."

"I could never have lived with myself if I didn't at least try. So I went to Galveston to be tested."

"Annnnddd??????"

"And . . . the news was great. Lynsey and I were a match!"

"Oh, my goodness," I commented with a smile. "I bet Becky was delirious with happiness."

"She was, she was. She cried with relief and gratitude, but our joy was short-lived. After some further testing, the coordinator canceled the transplant. As it turned out, due to her deteriorating condition requiring blood transfusions, the puzzle pieces of our blood cells would no longer line up well enough to risk the transplant."

"Oh, no. You all must have been completely devastated— and after such hopes!"

"It was horrible. I'll never forget the day we received the news that we couldn't proceed. We were sitting in the playroom of the children's hospital, sitting around a child-sized table in pint-sized chairs. Me, Ed and Becky, Lynsey's grandparents, and the surgeon. Becky is a fighter, she cried and begged the surgeon to please think of some other way to save her baby. The surgeon finally broke down and cried, too, saying, 'Becky if there was *any* way I could, you know that I would.'"

At this point, Melissa brushed away a tear. "All of us grown-ups sitting in these tiny chairs, helpless as small children to change Lynsey's fate. It was one of the saddest days I think I've ever lived through."

By this time, a lump formed in my own throat and I swallowed hard, waiting for Melissa to gather her thoughts and continue the story.

"After that, the only hope for prolonging Lynsey's life was the dreaded dialysis. A tube had to be surgically inserted in her abdomen. After a few weeks, she was able to go home from the hospital, but each night, for eight hours, she'd have to be hooked up to a dialysis machine. We all went through a grieving process, knowing this would only temporarily hold off the inevitable. She had the operation to insert the tube in July, then one day in August as I was vacuuming at home, I received a call from the transplant coordinator at UTMC."

"Yes?" I prodded, now literally on the edge of my seat.

"She said, 'Melissa, there's a new machine, at the University of Alabama—only one of its kind, and it has the ability to go deeper into the makeup of the blood cells. There's a slight chance that with this new technology, we might help yours and Lynsey's blood match after all.'"

I rested my head on my hand. "What an emotional roller coaster."

Melissa nodded. "You're not kidding. My first thought was, 'Can any of us take this again? The buildup of hope? The potential for more devastation?' We'd just about come to peace with the last round of bad news. But I had no choice, I knew we had to try. So I went to a nearby lab and they mailed off a sample of my blood to Alabama for testing."

"Two days later, I returned home from grocery shopping and Michael met me at the door, his eyes wide. He only said three words—'It's on, Melissa'—before I collapsed in his arms with relief, followed by panic. We had so much to get together and only twenty-four hours before the operation was scheduled to take place.

"We scrambled for airplane tickets and called my brother to come keep our kids, including Jordan. Then I canceled meetings . . ."

I laughed and said, "I can just hear you, Melissa. 'I'm sorry I won't be at the PTO bake sale, I'll be in the hospital giving a kidney next week.'"

Melissa smiled. "Actually, I was surprisingly calm during all the drama. The coordinators for transplants are wonderful; they make sure the donor has an advocate, that I knew all the risks involved. They even gave me a psychological exam."

"What kind of questions did they ask you?"

"This one psychologist asked me what I expected to get out of giving away my kidney. I couldn't help saying, 'Um, let's see . . . could it possibly be a *healthy child*?' Thankfully he had a good sense of humor and marked me down as 'sane.' One of the best things coming from this whole experience was knowing that yes, I have the strength to overcome my fears to help someone in need. People always wonder if they have it in them to help save someone's life. Now I know I do, and that's a wonderful feeling. Something no one can ever take away."

I was seized by a sudden and fierce admiration as I looked my friend full in the face and declared, "I am so proud of you."

"Thank you, that means a lot to me." Melissa lowered her eyes and brushed away a tear. "I think you would do the same."

I hope so, I thought, *I really hope so.*

I asked to see Melissa's scar. She lifted her shirt to reveal an incision about twelve inches long, encircling her lower waist from her midsection to the middle of her back.

"It's so long!" I exclaimed as I touched the thin line of scarred tissue.

"Yeah, "Melissa agreed. "They practically have to cut you in half, though now the procedure is much less invasive. The recovery period is typically longer for the donor than for the recipient. But it was all worth it when I saw Lynsey getting better each day. That is, until she began rejecting my kidney."

"Oh, no!"

"Yes. I never cried, never broke down during the whole process, but when they told me Lynsey was rejecting the kidney, and I realized we may have gone through this ordeal for nothing, I bawled like a baby."

Just hearing this story secondhand had me ping-ponging from one emotion to another, I couldn't begin to imagine how Melissa, Lynsey, and her family lived through these turbulent days.

"Again," Melissa continued, "we were given a shred of hope by some rare medical breakthrough. The specialists put Lynsey on some kind of new, strong medication—some concoction with monkey cells—to try to counteract the effects of rejection. Lynsey was the first child ever to receive this medication. In fact, Lynsey was among the first children at the University of Texas Medical Center in Galveston to receive a nonrelated kidney—so she's something of a landmark case there."

"Melissa," I said, "just listening to this sounds like a movie of the week."

"With the happiest of endings, because Lynsey got well. One hundred percent recovery. Within the next year, Becky and I were sitting in her living room laughing and talking when suddenly we saw my daughter Sarah's head peek up over the kitchen counter. Sarah was about five years old at the time. The next thing we knew, Lynsey's tiny four-year-old fist appeared, grabbing hold of Sarah's suspenders and pulling her down to the floor in a wrestling match. That was one skirmish between kids we were delighted to witness."

"Between your go-get'em kidney and those monkey blood cells—how could Lynsey *not* be spunky?" I asked with a grin. I paused, then searching Melissa's eyes, I quietly asked, "Do you realize how special you are?"

"You know," she answered slowly, truthfully, "I think I'd kind of forgotten. The last year has been so discouraging, it's been a while since someone's reminded me."

I asked Melissa if I could contact Becky, Lynsey's mom, and she agreed. Last night, I placed a call to Austin.

"I am so glad you are writing about this," Becky said with enthusiasm the moment I shared why I'd called. "Not a day goes by that I don't think of Melissa. It's like she is always near my heart, some part of me is saying a perpetual prayer of gratitude. I mean, how do you thank someone for giving you a healthy child?"

It's an emotion-filled question, but I knew what Melissa's answer to that would be.

"Becky," I replied. "Melissa never wants you to have a thought of obligation. She received so much from the whole experience, her joy is in knowing Lynsey is okay. By the way, how is our miracle girl doing?"

"She's pitching for her softball team, and driving all of us crazy at times, as only an active nine-year-old can. And we love her more than life itself. Right after the transplant, I wrote a letter to Oprah Winfrey, hoping there might be some way Melissa and I and Lynsey could appear on the show to share what this experience has meant to all of us—and encourage others to consider organ donation. I have a bumper sticker that reads, 'Don't take your kidneys to heaven, heaven knows we need them here.'"

"It's amazing how all these donation drives and walkathons for medical research take new meaning when our loved ones are affected," I commented.

"Isn't that the truth?" Becky agreed. "The hardest thing for us to contemplate is that, without a medical breakthrough, we may have to go through this again. The longest a kidney transplant has lasted so far is twenty years—and counting."

"Then we'll pray for a breakthrough," I said. "And so will everyone who reads of this story, I'm sure."

Becky faxed me the copy of her letter to Oprah. Unfortunately she and Melissa were not asked on the show, but I am so very proud to have them appear in this book. What an honor, what an inexplicable honor, to share their story of love, giving, and hope.

Recently Melissa wrote a letter to Ann Landers in response to a sibling concerned about donating her kidney. Because I felt it would be helpful to hear her post-donor feelings, she agreed to let me share her anonymous letter here:

Dear Ann Landers:

While there is always a risk involved in any surgical procedure, you must understand that kidney donation surgery is only performed on a very healthy patient. Since donating a kidney, my remaining kidney has functioned better than my two kidneys functioned before . . .

The first live-donation kidney transplant was performed over thirty years ago. The donor is still healthy and I know of no cases in which a donor's health was compromised by giving a kidney.

As to fear of death during or after surgery: the Bible says there is no greater love than to give your life for a friend. My faith allayed my fears. I had a feeling of absolute peace and certainty when I made this decision. That thought carried me through.

Next to giving birth to my two children, donating my kidney was the most rewarding experience of my life. The little girl who received my kidney was two and a half. She is now a healthy nine-year-old. This is my ultimate reward.

A Healthy Donor in Texas

Don't you just love happy endings?

Lynsey plays ball, 1997, 8 years old.

On Organ Donation

To Remember Me
by Robert N. Test

Don't call this my deathbed. Let it be called the Bed of Life, and let my body be taken from it to help others lead fuller lives.

Give my sight to a man who has never seen a sunrise, a baby's face, or love in the eyes of a woman. Give my heart to a person whose own heart has caused nothing but endless days of pain.

Give my blood to the teenager who was pulled from the wreckage of his car, so that he might live to see his grandchildren play. Give my kidneys to one who depends on a machine to exist. Take my bones, every muscle, every fiber and nerve in my body and find a way to make a crippled child walk.

Explore every corner of my brain. Take my cells, if necessary, and let them grow so that, someday, a speechless boy will shout at the crack of a bat and a deaf girl will hear the sound of rain against her window.

Burn what is left of me, and scatter the ashes to the winds to help the flowers grow.

If you must bury something, let it be my faults, weaknesses, and all prejudice against my fellow man.

If, by chance, you wish to remember me, do it with a kind deed or word to someone who needs you. If you do all I asked, I will live forever.[1]

Deprive someone of love, and you
deprive them of the very core of life itself.
—Anabel Gillham

A Bouquet of Love

*A*nabel.

It's the sort of name you want to pause and tip your hat to. A sweet Southern morning kind of name.

Fittingly, it was a bright May morning, when I pulled my red van into the driveway of Bill and Anabel Gillham's ranch style home at the edge of Fort Worth, Texas. I'd been waiting a long time for this moment. I'd never met Anabel face-to-face, though I'd been mothered and mentored by her words for the past few years.

Before I could even knock, the door flung open and out walked Bill, a mustached charmer of a gentlemen, to greet me. I entered the big friendly kitchen and eventually fell into a hug from Anabel, a pretty picture of a Southern lady, aged to perfection. She had soft peaks of white hair, tender blue eyes, and a drawl as low and soothing as a lullaby. But before I could get to Anabel I had to go through Bo.

Bo was quite possibly the ugliest dog I have ever laid eyes on. He looked too big to be hovering so low to the ground, like a dining room table cut off at the knees. He was the color of a slightly rusted iron skillet. I couldn't begin to guess the mixture of breeds from which he might have descended.

"I've never seen a dog like this," I offered as kindly as I could.

"And you never will," laughed Bill as he tugged the big lump of happy dog out of the way, "he's one of a kind."

"Love us, love our dog," Anabel chimed in, half laughing, half apologizing. And it was then I knew, without doubt, that I'd come to the right place. For as I glanced at poor ugly Bo, and back at the sentimental look on Anabel's face as she stroked his old coat, I knew I'd just entered a house of unconditional love.

I first heard of Bill and Anabel by way of an interview. Ironically, I was the one being interviewed. Mike Middleton, a man with a rich voice and welcoming face, sat across the radio microphone from me, asking the questions. He was an author's dream; he had actually *read* my book under discussion. Once the show ended, I reached out to shake Mike's hand, thanking him for a job well done—and I meant it. A DJ can make a person sound as brilliant as Einstein or as dense as Ernest. Today, Mike had helped this nervous country girl to shine.

"Becky," Mike said as he gathered up his notes, "have you ever heard of Bill and Anabel Gillham?"

"No, I can't say that I have."

"You ought to meet them. From hearing you talk today about how much you respect people who are transparent, I just have a feeling you'd love them."

"Why is that?"

"I work with Bill and Anabel on a radio program; I've known them for years. Their love for each other and for others amazes me. In ministry I've seen people suddenly change as soon as the spotlight hits them or the microphone comes on. Bill and Anabel are the most consistently real and loving people I know.

Onstage or off. I always walk away from them feeling like I've been dipped in love."

Mike directed me to one of Anabel's books and recommended I order a tape series from the Gillham's ministry, which I did.

When the series arrived on a summer day, I popped the first tape in our living room stereo and listened as I folded laundry. Bill spoke first. If Anabel's voice is a lullaby, Bill's was a hoedown. A licensed psychologist, Dr. Gillham understands the complicated inner workings of the mind, but as a country boy from Oklahoma he knows how to convey deep truths in terms any Southerner can warm to. "Now gang," he'd say in his homespun style, "our bodies are just our 'earth suits,' but who we really are is 'spirit critters.' Ya see, we're spirit critters having an earth suit experience."

He talked of how we were created to want love, how we long for it with every fiber of our being. How it wasn't until mid-life that he realized the extent of God's love for him. Sadly, by then he'd wreaked twenty years of havoc in his marriage. After Bill finished his introduction, Anabel began to speak. She unfolded a tale of her days as a young wife who performed her whole life trying to be the total Christian woman in an effort to please Bill and God. (And trying to keep straight who was who.) Bill specialized in shooting cutting remarks and sharp criticisms in Anabel's direction. "His game, back then," she said without laughing, "was 'Let's Destroy Anabel.'"

Added to the pain of her husband's criticism, Anabel was a perfectionist with a hypersensitive spirit. The combination proved to be too much: depressive thoughts filled her mind, her steps grew heavy, her body weary. Then one day God met Anabel in the kitchen through an experience with one of her three sons. Mason, their youngest child, was born profoundly retarded with a myriad of medical problems. Eventually they had to make the agonizing decision to put him in an institutional facility, but one weekend, during a visit at home, something divinely simple occurred.

Anabel was washing dishes when, in a moment of internal turmoil and anguish, she suddenly stopped, got down on her knees in front of Mason, took his dirty little hands in hers and . . . well, I'll let Anabel tell the rest.

"'Mason,' I said to my precious child, 'I love you. I love you. If only you could understand how much I love you.' He just stared. He couldn't understand; he didn't comprehend. I stood up and started on the dishes again, but that didn't last long. This sense of urgency—almost a panic—came over me, and once more I dried my hands and knelt in front of my precious little boy.

"'My dear Mason, if only you could say to me, "I love you, Mother." I need that, Mase.'

"Nothing.

"I stood up to the sink again. More dishes, more washing, more crying—and thoughts foreign to my way of thinking began filtering into my conscious awareness. I believe God spoke to me that day, and this is what He said: 'Anabel, you don't look at your son and turn away in disgust because he's sitting there with saliva drooling out of his mouth; you don't shake your head, repulsed because he has dinner all over his shirt or because he's sitting in a dirty, smelly diaper when he ought to be able to take care of himself. Anabel, you don't reject Mason because all the dreams you had for him have been destroyed. You don't reject him because he doesn't perform for you. You love him, Anabel, just because he is yours. Mason doesn't willfully reject your love, but you willfully reject Mine. I love you, Anabel, not because you're neat or attractive, not because you do things well, not because you perform for Me, but just because you're mine.'"

This revelation was incredible to Anabel, who had struggled

for so many years, hating her performance patterns, "yet living to perform, driven to perform, searching out the praise of men and thirsting for the love of God I thought could come only to those who performed well enough to receive it." She didn't have to do anything for God, didn't even have to *be* something for Him. In a way that Anabel could understand, God showed her that He loved her *as is*—just because she was His.

When my children were toddlers, I'd sometimes catch them running through the house and suddenly be caught up by their beauty. I'd sneak up, take one of them in my arms and say, "Hey, kiddo, I love you! Do you know that?" Anabel Gillham had caught me running through the living room of my life, surprised me with this recorded embrace of words, slowing me down with her unguarded story of love. At this point in my own life, my rickety ladder of performance-based acceptance had begun to shake and rattle. Anabel's story hit close to home. I clicked off the tape, slowly walked out the back door where I sank into the porch swing, put my head in my hands and wept.

"Lord," I cried, "look at this mess of myself—I'm not doing life well. Oh, I put on a good show. But inside, I'm overwhelmed at every turn trying to be who I cannot be. I've fallen below all the standards I've set for myself and I'm worn out with the effort. I don't understand why You love me, but I'm ready to accept that You are a God who loves messed up people with nothing to offer You but empty hands." And He came and soothed me with His spirit, filling my empty hands with buckets of undeserved love.

Interestingly, God didn't send an angel to touch Anabel with news of His love. He met Anabel—dishpan hands and all—in the kitchen, through the wordless response from a retarded child. He didn't meet me in a stained glass cathedral, He met me on a porch swing, using Anabel's story. I was beginning to see a free-spirited side to God's love. We can never guess how or where He'll show up.

Though I felt great relief at having faced my inadequacy and having met God's open arms, there was still an area I continued to struggle with. Within a few days of my prayer on the porch swing I was lying on my bed face up, crying tears in my ears. (I cried a lot in my mid-thirties. From what I read and hear from my friends, it's a fairly common occurrence. Take note if you are approaching ages thirty-three through thirty-seven, stock up on Kleenex.) I'd just had an argument with my husband, Scott, and my marriage seemed to be stuck in an unending pattern. Get along two weeks, fight one week, get along two weeks, fight one more. I was as desperately tired of this pattern as I'd been of my own personal struggles to be perfect.

I wanted to relax and hold hands with our marriage. I wanted us to lean into one another the way some old couples do who know they are truly one in the most mysterious of ways—not just two people walking the same path because it's the right thing to do.

"Okay, God," I wailed internally, "You know I've read 106 books on how to make a marriage grow up and fly right. We've gone to counseling. We've filled out personality graphs. I've even tried the 'seduce him in Saran Wrap' trick. What else do you want me to DO?" At that moment, I reached over and picked up Anabel's book from the nightstand. *The Confident Woman. Hmmm . . .* As I randomly flipped the pages, it fell to a chapter where Anabel described a technique she uses to "let go of burdens." It involved releasing a helium balloon to the sky—as a symbol of giving a problem to God—then recording the released burden on a piece of paper and keeping it in a dated envelope.

As I scanned the page my eyes fell on Anabel's written words: "In complete desperation . . . I gave my son to the Lord." The next line caused me to swallow hard. "I have an envelope to prove that I did. It has 'June 27, 1976 A.M. GOD' written on the outside."

June 27, 1976. June 27, 1976! On the very same day and year that Anabel was giving her son's medical condition to the Lord, Scott and I stood trembling before an altar, two teenagers with more hormones than brains, repeating vows that would bind us together forever—and prove impossible to live up to. (I have a friend who says there should be a country song called "I Said 'I Do' but I Don't Think We Did.")

I was truly stunned. Sure, I had just asked God what He wanted me to do, but I'd meant it more like a rhetorical prayer. I certainly didn't expect to have Him answer me so clearly—and quickly. But as I read about letting go, and stared at our wedding date written on the page in front of me—I couldn't deny this was a God Thing. He may as well have picked up a megaphone, put it to my ear and shouted: "Here's a little hint for you, Becky: Let Go. Give Up. Helium your efforts and let Me have your marriage."

Again, God used Anabel's words to touch me, across time and space, at what psychologists call "the precise point of felt need."

Not long after that afternoon, Scott took me out to dinner. As we sipped coffee, he paused and looked me full in the face. "Becky," he began, "I just want to tell you that I am so sorry for the pain I've caused in our marriage. I want to become better friends, closer lovers . . ." His words were an unsolicited gift of grace, allowing me to open my heart, to confess my own failures as a wife and solidify our love. I'd done nothing to pull or manipulate Scott into this offering. I'd simply let go of the struggle. It would be the first of many times I would discover that God does amazingly well without my help.

Anabel placed a plate of her special tuna salad in front of Bill and me as we sat at the small kitchen table overlooking the pretty backyard. A bird flew into view. Anabel noted its presence with gratitude. Bill led us in a simple prayer of thanks.

"Anabel," I said, as I reached for a glass of iced tea, "I want you to know what a privilege this is, to finally meet you. God's used your written and recorded words in the most uncanny ways in my life that I feel like you've been my friend over the years."

Anabel smiled and, I swear, she lit up the kitchen with her radiance. Love does incredible things with a face. Her tender countenance reminded me of a question

"Do you mind if I ask you something?" I ventured. She shook her head, curious.

"Okay. The other day. On the phone. When I asked if I might come over and meet you. Do you remember how, before I said good-bye, you said—'And Becky, I love you.'"

"Yes," Anabel nodded.

"But Anabel, how could you say that? You don't even know me."

"Oh, yes. Oh yes, I do," she replied without hesitation. "I probably know you better than you know yourself. Because I know what Jesus thinks of you, Becky. I know how precious you are to Him, I know that you are the apple of His eye. So I do know you, and I do love you. With all my heart."

When I'm in my seventh decade, as Anabel is, I hope I am filling my days the way this woman is—catching people in hugs of unconditional love as they happen by.

Our time together that warm afternoon ended all too quickly. After closing in prayer, Anabel walked me to the door and stood in the driveway waving goodbye.

"I love you, Becky," she said again. As I backed out of the driveway—trying to avoid taking the mailbox with me—I caught a glimpse of her reaching down to give Bo a good scratching behind the ears.

Me and Bo, basking in Anabel's unconditional love.

My cup—and Bo's bowl—runneth over.[1]

On Unconditional Love

"This sounds very simple and maybe even trite, but very few people know that they are loved without any conditions or limits."[2]

—*Henri Nouwen*

"There is no surprise more magical than the surprise of being loved. It is the finger of God on a man's shoulder."[3]

—*Charles Morgan*

"To be manifestly loved, to be openly admired are human needs as basic as breathing. Why, then, wanting them so much ourselves, do we deny them so often to others?"[4]

—*Arthur Gordon, A Touch of Wonder*

"I feel that all disease is ultimately related to a lack of love, or to love that is only conditional . . . I also feel that all healing is related to the ability to give and accept unconditional love."[5]

—*Dr. Bernie Siegal*

"Things are beautiful if you love them."[6]

—*Jean Anouilh*

"I have loved you with an everlasting love;
. . . with lovingkindness I have drawn you."

—*Our Heavenly Father (Jeremiah 31:3 NKJV)*

I was twenty, my life was in turmoil, and I hungered for a visit with Grandma—along with a plateful of speckled butter beans.
—Rose McCray

A Resilient Rose Garden

Y ou want to have our coffee inside the house, or down in the trees?"

"Down in the trees sounds lots more interesting," I answered my friend, Rose McCray. Picking up a steaming crystal cup and saucer, I caught a whiff of the fragrant morning elixir before taking the cherished first sip of the day.

"Your house smells like my grandmother Nonnie's kitchen," I mused aloud as I follow Rose through the living room toward the back door.

Often when I'm with Rose I feel as though I've journeyed to a bygone era, though she is actually younger than I am. With porcelain skin, eyes the color of robin eggs and long, golden-red curls, Rose could easily be a cover model for *Victoria* magazine or a living cameo.

We walked down the wooden steps and to a spot of trees nestled at the edge of the seventeen acres that Rose and her husband, Fred, call their homestead

Two hammocks swung side-by-side invitingly, but we sat on chairs pulled up to a table made of graying wood, speckled with faded green paint.

"Where'd you get this great old table?" I asked.

"Found it on the road," Rose answered. "Someone had just thrown it away, but I thought it had character. I love old stuff."

"I know what you mean. 'Old' can be kind of comforting." I pointed to an intriguing patch of dying vegetation. "Is that your garden?"

Rose laughed, and as she did, soft tresses of honey-colored curls bounced and swayed behind her. "Yes, such as it is. You should have seen it this spring, before the summer heat wave zapped it. I like a garden to grow tall and wild and free. Back home in Louisiana, I used to love wandering through my grandma's garden. It was this giant jungle wonderland of tomatoes, butter beans, purple hull peas, collard greens . . ."

I nodded, remembering how I loved watching my Nonnie work her flower beds when I was a small child.

Rose appeared wistful as she stared over the tops of the dried cornstalks. "Grandma loved and prayed me through so many hard times. So I call this my 'heirloom garden' in her memory." After a brief pause, she smiled and added, "Of course I'm not sure she'd want to claim it the way it looks right now. You'll have to come back next spring."

"It's a date," I said as my eyes followed a unique border around the garden's edge. "I love that fencing. Did you make it?"

"Yes! It's called waddling and it's not hard to do, just time consuming. You jab some rough tree branch sticks in the ground, about two to three feet apart, and then weave sticks and vines in and out between them in stacks."

"It's beautiful, kind of like a handwoven rug fence." I took a deep breath of country air on that first morn of September. The sun backlighted Rose's hair, framing her face like a halo of angel fire. Birdsong punctuated the air as a light breeze played about the leaves and grass. I positioned myself where the late summer, early fall sky would paint just the right amount of sunlight onto my face and arms.

Between the two of us, Rose and I have eight children: their ages range from eighteen down to ten in stair step order and the whole lot of them are good friends. That day our kids had gone off to school in our small town of Lone Oak. (I call it a "one tree" kind of town.) We had been busy summertime moms, and both of us treasured this rare moment of uninterrupted coffee and conversation.

When Rose McCray and her family first moved to our neck of the woods a couple of years ago, our family was thrilled to discover they were outdoor enthusiasts who loved rock climbing, mountain hiking, and sailing. It's tough to find folks who enjoy any sports beyond football and "varmint hunting" in our rural redneck community, so Scott and my boys, especially, were glad to have some adventure-oriented companions.

Rose is quite the outdoorswoman, though I must admit, I'm not a sportswoman of any kind. I don't do rocks, mountains, ships, football, or varmints. Even so, we found we had plenty in common. We both love reading, writing, cheering our kids, and old-fashioned back porch visiting. It didn't take many visits to realize Rose was a remarkable woman of faith, with an amazing story to tell.

I knew something of Rose's background before coming to this picnic-like coffee on the grounds. In the months of our slowly evolving friendship, Rose shared that she married—at the tender age of seventeen—a twenty-one-year-old man named Kyle (not his real name), who was a new convert to Christianity. He was zealous for God, a lay minister in their Pentecostal church home, the denomination of Rose's childhood. Sadly, his story strangely paralleled the preacher played by Robert Duvall in the movie, *The Apostle*.

Kyle's zeal for church, and his true compassion for the people in it, had a fatal flaw that ultimately sent his life plummeting; he was, to put it in politically correct terms, *morally impaired*.

The year Rose turned twenty, she went away for an extended period of time to comfort and nurse her thirty-nine-year-old mother who was dying of cancer. Upon her return, she discovered that Kyle had been unfaithful. Her heart broke into a million pieces, but even though Rose felt like an unwitting character in a tragic soap opera, somehow her faith remained strong. And this was only the beginning of the stranger-than-fiction events that would unfold in her life. That morning I'd gone to hear, as Paul Harvey says, "the rest of the story," but mostly, I wanted to discover how the backbone of Rose's faith kept her from breaking in those hurricanes.

My coffee cup made a quiet clinking sound as I placed it carefully on the saucer in front of me. "What did you do when you discovered Kyle's betrayal?"

"I spent lots of nights in prayer, lying prostrate, face down in the carpet," Rose answered truthfully. "My human reaction was just what you'd imagine—I was hurt, angry, jealous, terrified. But whenever I was in prayer, offering up my honest feelings to God, not holding anything back, just yielding to Him, I knew I wouldn't have to walk through this alone. Not once do I ever remember feeling abandoned by God. He was always there, loving me, strengthening me as He'd done since I was a child."

"After the emotional winds began to settle, how did you deal with those who had wronged you?" I asked.

"I confronted my husband, and the women involved. To my shock, there had been more than one woman. I've never been one to back away or run from a problem. Believing that all things are possible with God's help, I was open to reconciliation with my husband, who seemed genuinely repentant. One by one, over time, I forgave those who'd hurt me by drawing on the Scriptures and prayer. It wasn't easy; it was gradual. And I never felt that I was doing the forgiving; it was Christ loving and forgiving them through me. Even now, years later, people tell me how they saw God's grace acted out in my willingness to forgive."

"How did you *do* that?" I asked with amazement. "How could you forgive so many, for so much?"

"Becky," Rose explained, "It wasn't all for their sake. It was for my own sake as well. Hatred and bitterness would only destroy me, and then what? I've never been able to judge people, even my husband or the women who acted like harlots in this case. I've always been keenly aware of God's grace toward me; there's nothing good in me that isn't from Him. As a child I used to feel so alone sometimes, but whenever I'd pray I felt assured that God was watching over me."

"Why did you feel alone?" I wondered aloud.

"My mom and dad had terrible, violent fights; eventually they separated and divorced. My mother basically abandoned me at my grandmother's house when I was nine years old. That's one of the reasons I was so close to my grandma. Though I don't remember it, my grandmother told me I'd sit and cry for hours, begging for my mom. What I do remember is going to church; sometimes I'd even ride the church bus to get there, all by myself. Often I went to the hour-long prayer meetings before the services."

"I'm trying to imagine a young girl sitting and praying for that length of time . . ."

"I know it sounds strange, but I loved praying. For me it was a source of tremendous comfort. Sometimes in prayer, I'd relive vivid memories of sad times, but as I did I would also feel God holding me close, helping me cope."

"Neither of my parents were walking with God back then," Rose said. "I learned how to hold my emotions together, but it's like I instinctively knew I didn't have to be so strong when I was with God. So I always stayed vulnerable with Him.

"Eventually, my father remarried and within a couple years, he and my stepmother dedicated their lives to God and took me to live with them. That made a huge positive difference. One day, when I was about fifteen, I was praying and suddenly realized, with great relief, that I could think back on my childhood hurts without aching inside. I didn't cry any more after that, not over the past."

"Do you feel like God was parenting you in a way?"

"Yes, and as I look back I see He was also very much my counselor. When I didn't know what to do, He was, as Isaiah says, the Wonderful Counselor."

I remember reading that Christianity is one of the only religions, of all the religions in the world, that has a word for *father*—and remarkably, that word was personalized even more when Jesus said we could call God the familiar Aramaic term, *Abba*—our Western equivalent of Daddy or Papa. There are many reasons I cling to Christianity as truth, but this is one that's at the top of my list. Like Rose, I need a God who is also my loving heavenly Parent, a God I can get my arms around when the lights go out.

"So, Rose," I prodded, my mind back on the story at hand, "what happened after you forgave Kyle for his unfaithfulness?"

"I struggled to make our marriage work. But a couple of years later, when I was nearly nine months pregnant, I discovered Kyle was having another affair, this time with a friend of mine. It was devastating to everyone involved; the 'other woman' and her husband, Fred, had three little preschoolers."

"And you were about to have your first baby!?!"

Rose McCray nodded. "But it was the strangest thing, Becky. I didn't break, not this time. For my baby's sake, I refused to go to pieces emotionally. I was determined to carry my baby to term with dignity, and God gave me a peace beyond understanding. Two days after I found out about the affair, I gave birth to my beautiful daughter at home with a midwife—and named her Hope."

"A fitting name," I said with a smile, imagining Rose cradling new life, the universal symbol of hope. "Where was Kyle when Hope was born?"

"He was at the birth, out of obligation, but within a week, he was gone. Even as I struggled with the pain of watching my husband walk away from me and our newborn into the arms of another woman, once again, in prayer, I had this precious assurance that the Lord would be my Husband. Now, I am a forgiving person, but I am not stupid. This time, for my sake and my daughter's sake—" For the first time since Rose began sharing her tale, tears sprang to her eyes and her voice broke.

"This time, it was so precious. The Lord assured me He'd be with me whatever I chose to do: hope and work for reconciliation again, or let Kyle go and start my life as a single mother. With all trust gone, I didn't have the strength to fight to keep a one-sided marriage."

"So, what happened next?" I couldn't help myself. Hearing Rose's story was like reading a novel where the heroine is caught in a web of tragic events and left dangling at the end of the chapter. I desperately wanted the good guy—or in this case, the good girl—to win.

"Well," Rose picked up the story threads and began again. "The other woman's husband was a good, kind, godly man, and when our spouses ran off together, she left those three adorable children behind in his care. I'd known him from a distance, though we'd never been close friends."

"And how old were their children again?"

"Let's see, Omny was six, Walker was four, and Hannah was two."

"Go on . . ."

"Well, as you can imagine, Fred McCray and I found some comfort in knowing each of us understood the other's pain. As we waded through the agonies and legalities of watching our marriages dissolve, a solid friendship grew between us. I adored his children and he felt the same way about baby Hope. It wasn't a wildly passionate kind of falling in love, but more of a beautiful, gradual knowing that we wanted to be together as husband and wife, to raise our children under one roof, to have the only thing we'd both ever really wanted: a whole, complete, intact family."

"What did the people at church think of your announcement to marry?"

"Actually my pastor and his wife were, and are, good friends, and they thought I would end up being in some kind of full-time ministry someday. When I told them I planned to marry Fred and be a stay-at-home mom they said, 'Rose we'd hoped you'd marry someone who would enhance your ministry.' At that point, I'd had my fill of 'ministers,' and told them, 'I don't want to be *enhanced*, I want to be *romanced*!'"

I laughed at Rose's honesty, then brushed away a stray bug before it decided to take a nose dive into my coffee. "You know this is a pretty incredible story . . ."

"Even more incredible was the day that the judge gave Fred custody of all the children, which is highly unusual in the state of Texas, where children nearly always go to the biological mother. I was twenty-three years old when we married, and an instant mother to four preschoolers!"

"Whoa. I bet that was a tough transition for you newlyweds."

"Yeah, but I LOVED it, Becky. Sure it was hard, terribly hard, but Fred's children were like my own from the beginning. There's no difference in our love for them. Everything we'd do, every decision we made, we'd ask ourselves, 'What's best for the kids?' They were, and are, our number one priority. I knew too well how it felt to be shuffled to the back of parents' agendas. I never want our kids to doubt their value to us."

I couldn't help thinking about radio psychologist and child advocate, Dr. Laura, who begins every show by stating with pride, "I am my kid's mom." Fred and Rose would make Dr. Laura stand up and applaud. They are, without apology, their kids' parents.

"They obviously love you both," I affirmed. "It's so much fun to watch your family together. You've got a great bunch of kids. How long have you and Fred been married now?"

"Ten years!" At this point Rose's voice filled with emotion, "And look at the blessing! Look at the gold that came out of the fire—the love in our home! When I look around at this place He's given us, and the goodness He's showered on me, the joy is sometimes overwhelming. Another side story: after Fred and I married I had to have a hysterectomy. I'd always dreamed of a big family, and my chance for more children of my own was gone. But God gave me the desires of my heart when He allowed me to mother Omny, Walker, and Hannah along with Hope."

"Your faith amazes me," I confessed, wondering how I would have handled the trials that Rose endured. Not as well, I decided, honestly. "Do you ever struggle with doubt?"

"Oh, sure, I doubt God sometimes. I'm no saint. But every time I've really struggled with questions about God's reality or His concern for me, He reassures me of His care.

"One time I was in church with the thought going through my head, 'What do you think of me, God? I feel like a nothing. What do You see when You look down at me?' I wasn't crying, wasn't calling any attention to myself, just a silent question. At that moment, the pastor suddenly stopped his sermon, walked down the aisle took me by the hand, and said, 'You are God's daughter, His most precious one. As the gold in Fort Knox is protected, so He will watch over and protect you.'"

"You know, Rose, if I write that, some people may say, 'That's a generic blessing that could apply to anyone.'"

"And I'd say, 'You may be right.' But I, alone, knew the silent question my own heart was asking that night. I, alone, believe God answered that question in a way that reached down and enveloped me with His love. It's not the kind of thing I'd put up for debate; it's too personal. My 'knower' knows that I know, that I know, that I know: God sees me. And—mess that I sometimes am—He loves me. He's used all kinds of ways to encourage me. Sometimes it's a scripture, sometimes a song, and sometimes comfort comes, yes, through loving, imperfect saints at church."

I look at my watch and cannot believe how much time had passed since we first walked into this garden grove. "I hate to say this, but I've to get going." Slowly I stretched, stood up, and brushed a few leaves off my jeans. My eyes were drawn again to the garden and I commented, "Your grandmother would be proud of you, Rose."

"All the glory goes to God, if that is true. I've been writing down some of my memories of Grandma lately. Someday I'd love to write a book about her gardening techniques, along with her techniques for just plain good living."

"I wish I could have known her. May I take something you've written to read later today?"

Within a few minutes, I drove away from Rose's wilderness home with my insides made happy by good coffee and deep conversation, my outsides warmed by the sun, and memories of a gardening grandma tucked into my notebook.

After completing several errands in town, I drove home and wandered out to my own front porch swing. Opening my notebook, I pulled out the pages Rose had given me and began getting more acquainted with a grandmother and the child, now woman, who loved her.

In Search of Grandma's Garden
by Rose McCray

The fresh dew glistening in the sunlight and the music of waking birds signaled that Grandma would not be sitting idly in the house. Oh no, not Grandma. On such a fine spring morning she would be found tending her garden or digging a new flower bed. Wasting such a morning would be close to sin as far as she was concerned. I was twenty, my life was in turmoil, and I hungered for a visit with Grandma, along with a plateful of speckled butter beans.

Sure enough, as I approached her small white frame house, I saw her kneeling, transplanting touch-me-nots along the fence line. When I was a little girl, Grandma had allowed me to pick the little popping seed pods from these flowers with the funny sounding name. I remember carrying my treasure home in a small brown paper bag, feeling like Grandma's flower princess.

Watching Grandma work in her garden over the years was a pleasantly familiar scene. She always wore a big straw hat or sunbonnet to protect her fair skin from the harsh Louisiana sun, and light cotton clothing to keep cool. Her hands were never without her flower print gloves when she worked outside. She was a living portrait that appeared many times in my mind's eye, always soothing and cheering my heart.

As I watched Grandma rise from her beautiful bed of flowers, I knew she would have to retire from her beloved garden before long. Her movements were slow and pain-ridden, but still she greeted me with a generous smile and folded me inside her warm "grandma hug." Little did I know at the time how accurate my guess was. Grandma would be making heaven her home within a few short months of this day, which would turn out to be our last visit together.

The smell of breakfast still lingered as we entered the immaculate little house with hardwood floors and Naugahyde furniture. Smoked bacon, homemade biscuits and gravy, eggs, and of course, the savory smell of chicory coffee tempted my senses. It had been a long time since I'd come to Grandma's house, but as far as I could tell, thankfully, not much had changed. The old clock on the television

began to chime and as it rang through the kitchen, senti-
ment almost got the best of me.

"Let's take a look at my garden," Grandma finally
offered.

I thought she'd never ask.

As I looked up from my lap of Rose's journalings, I was reminded of how it is the old, well-known things we long for, and pil-
grimage to, in times of change and crisis. The chime of an old
clock on the black-and-white television, the smell of chicory coffee, the sight of familiar vines winding their way up decades-old
poles, Grandma's hug. These things, all together, made up the
haven that welcomed Rose whenever life grew cold and lonely
and unfamiliar. With her grandmother's prayers and love, Rose
discovered her own internal garden of continual hope.

As Albert Camus so aptly said, "In the midst of winter, I
found there was within me an invincible summer."

On the Joy of Gardening

(From the pages of Rose's journal)

"Yes, the sowing of a seed seems a very simple matter, but I always feel as if it were a sacred thing among the mysteries of God.

"Standing by that space of blank and motionless ground, I think of all it holds for me of beauty and delight, and I am filled with joy."

—*Celia Thaxter*

"God Almighty first planted a garden. And, indeed, it is the purest of human pleasures."

—*Francis Bacon*

"Apprentice yourself to nature. Not a day will pass without her opening a new and wondrous world of experience to learn from and enjoy."

—*Richard W. Langer*

"The Lord will guide you continually . . . you shall be like a watered garden."

Isaiah 58:11 NKJV

I love a challenge.
—Bernie Bland

A Lily in the Valley

"Whatever my lot, Thou hast taught me to say,
It is well, it is well, with my soul."[1]

Bernie should by all rights have aged prematurely, I thought as I made my way down the dirt path and through emerald foliage surrounding the jungle "boot camp." I was on my way to visit Bernie Bland, cofounder of the most unconventional (and possibly most effective) ministry I have ever seen: Teen Missions International. I'd arrived the night before in Merritt Island and couldn't wait to get to the familiar campgrounds and see how my old friends were faring.

I am always amazed how many adults I meet who have a teenage TMI summer adventure tucked away in their memories, as I do. When we find one another it sparks an immediate bond, as if we are sorority siblings with treasures of secrets in common.

In Bernie's forty-nine years as wife of Bob Bland—plumber-turned-pastor-turned visionary/missionary—she has experienced more excitement than most of us could amass in two lifetimes. She almost died from malaria; she was knocked unconscious in the jungles of Peru by an absentminded, oar-wielding teenager; and she has had her body invaded by a myriad of amoebas from foreign lands. She's cooked innumerable meals in gargantuan quantities over primitive fire pits, washed truckloads of used clothing to send to poverty-stricken children, and has comforted and encouraged thousands of teenagers far from home—and all without complaint.

To my way of thinking, the name *Bernie* should be found next to the word *trouper* in Webster's. Coleading an organization that has sent more than 34,000 Americans (and just as many third-world national teens) to serve various parts of the world would leave most of us dreaming of retirement. But retirement has never been in the Blands' long-range plans. They run an "ever onward, heave-ho" operation.

But this year had been different. December of 1997 had dealt Bernie the blow of a lifetime, and 1998, and all years to follow would never again be the same. I was concerned that I might find this resilient Floridian Magnolia without her bounce, resigned to a rocking chair.

I approached a cement-block dorm room and opened the door quietly. There Bernie lay napping on a bed. Mildly surprised, I could see that her recent ordeal had not aged her diminutive form nor whitened her curly dark hair. She seemed to me like a female Dick Clark: ever young.

"Bernie," I said softy, noticing her bandaged foot. I'd been told she'd had a recent surgery to correct a bone spur. But it was not her foot that concerned me today. It was her heart—that gentlest, most tender of hearts.

Sensing my presence she wearily said, "Becky." No more words following my name.

"Hey, you sweet lady," I responded, walking into the coolness of the darkened room. "How *are* you?"

"Oh, Honey, it's been a terrible year," she said.

"I know," I offered as I moved to her bed, blinking back tears. "I know."

I know, and yet—I do not know. How could I know what it was like to fall in love with an ebony-haired grandbaby named Joel, with eyes the color of rich mahogany and a smile as big as Christmas morning? I'd never *been* a grandmother. How could I know how it felt to watch this adorable boy grow to a young man so handsome and charming he magnetized rooms full of people— young and old alike—with his presence.

How could I possibly fathom what it was like to walk into a hospital emergency room and see this same grandson—captain of the football team—lying paralyzed from the neck down, a casualty of an impetuous dive into a too-shallow pool?

I tried to imagine Bernie holding hands with her family— grief-stricken Bob, her only son, Robin, her beloved daughter-in-law, Maxine, and granddaughter, Tara, as they encircled Joel, this man-child, this joy of their family. How she must have felt as she stood powerless to help, except to offer prayers and her presence, as they waited out the agonizing hours before Joel's spirit slipped from this earth to heaven's unseen welcome?

I knew, intellectually and emotionally, it had been a horrible year for Bernie and her family. But there's much more I didn't know, for how can any of us *really* know what we haven't ourselves yet survived? Reading medical journals about childbirth and actually pushing a ten-pound infant from my womb into the world had been two different things altogether. Observing a friend's grief, and actually facing the truth that our beloved has vanished from our daily lives, are continents of experience apart, separated by a sea of pain.

So as I wrote these words in my journal, I was acutely aware that trying to describe another's heartbreak—as empathetic as I felt—is not the same as "feeling my own heart shatter in my chest," the way Joel's mother described her anguish at Joel's passing.

Joel's mother, Bernie's daughter-in-law, is also my friend. Her name is Maxine, and twenty-four years ago I was fifteen, she seventeen. We hailed from the opposite ends of North America and met in the Florida swamplands of Teen Missions Boot Camp. Maxine breezed in from the crisp country of Canada. I moseyed to Merritt Island from Dallas with a slow Southern drawl. She called me "Tex," I called her "Max." We were friends from the very first day we giggled at each other's accents.

During our two weeks of survival camp training we'd joined hundreds of other kids under a Big Top tent for old-fashioned rally-type services each evening. Then, on the night of the commissioning ceremony, we all lit candles as symbols of commitment. The next morning we split into small teams, flying toward various countries across the globe to do our small part in saving the big world.

Two years later I married Scott, who'd also been on our team to El Salvador, and Maxine married Robin, Bob and Bernie's son. Joel was born to them soon after and then came Tara, their gorgeous, spunky (could she be otherwise?) daughter, now seventeen.

And twenty-four years later, I was back in Florida, having accepted an invitation to speak to 1,500 teens under the familiar Big Top, to share the incredible things God can do with one weak-kneed teenager in one adventure-filled summer.

Maxine and Robin had a home a short distance from the camp. They'd invited me to stay with them and I'd arrived late the night before. I was supremely grateful for their offer. I was afraid the alternative would be sleeping in a tent, swatting mosquitoes, and sweating miserably. (What seemed earthy and adventurous at fifteen, wasn't nearly as enticing at age thirty-nine.)

Maxine had greeted me warmly at the door, and for a few seconds we exchanged small talk. But then I spied Joel's laughing portrait on the wall, and I lost it. I held out my arms to Maxine and cried, "I am just so, so sorry. I can't believe you've had to live through this nightmare." Then we fell silent and just stood there hugging.

Moments later, we wiped at our tears and Maxine offered me a seat at the kitchen counter, managing to pour me a tall glass of soda. "Becky, I think there is possibly something worse than even what I've gone through. I think Bob and Bernie, as Joel's grandparents, may actually carry a heavier grief. Not only do they miss Joel fiercely, but they continue to mourn for our whole family: they hurt for me and Robin and Tara every day. It is like their heartache is multiplied."

I marveled at Maxine's benevolence in the midst of her own pain.

I glanced now at Maxine's mother-in-law. Bernie was right. Obviously, this had been a terrible year. I wondered if this tragedy would be the grand finale of the Blands' fruitful ministry? How could they find the strength to go on reaching out to others after all they'd been through? And yet . . .

A knock at Bernie's dorm room door interrupted my musings. Bob Bland poked his head inside, and I couldn't help but note how Bernie's tired eyes brightened at the sound of his voice.

"Bernie," Bob said, with the joy of a kid who has just tasted ice cream for the first time, "you've got to see this!"

Tempted by her husband's little-boy invitation, Bernie literally rose to the occasion. With only a slight limp, she walked out the door into the sunshine and beckoned me to follow her to the porch. There, about fifteen yards in front of us was a huge front-end loader, plunged face down in a small lake. Apparently, the shore had given way. The driver of the sinking machine, a volunteer named Curt Bitterman, stood nearby looking sheepish.

"So, Curt," Bob shouted with a wide grin, "is this the part where I'm supposed to say, 'I'm just glad you weren't hurt'?"

Curt only shook his head and headed to the jungle for rein-forcements. Within minutes men appeared with heavy chains and roaring equipment that looked amazingly like a giant col-lection of Tonka toys. Wide-eyed boys with wide-lens cameras swarmed out of the woods like ants drawn to frosting.

"We should sell popcorn," I commented. Bernie acknowl-edged my attempt at humor with a nod, but her dancing blue eyes were fixed on Bob, the corners of her mouth turning up in a slow smile.

"He looks good, doesn't he?" she asked with the admiration of a schoolgirl. I nodded. Bob was tanned, fit, with a head full of gorgeous silver hair. Indeed, no one would guess Bob Bland was seventy years old. "He just got his cast off yesterday," Bernie com-mented casually.

"What?!?" I asked in amazement.

"Yes, he broke his foot a couple of months ago."

"So you two have been limping around like twins?"

"I guess you could say that, but you know Bob. The day after he broke his foot he was riding his bike around here, his foot in a cast and his crutches laying across the handle bars."

"Bernie, I sure remember Bob's famous motto. I think it gave me the strength to survive natural childbirth. 'When the going gets tough—"

"—the tough get going.' Yep, and that man lives what he preaches."

Just then a roar of cheers erupted as the men successfully pulled the loader out of its embarrassing predicament.

In an odd moment of epiphany, I realized I was surrounded by resiliency everywhere I looked from this front porch perch. The front-end loader, only moments before, had appeared help-lessly, permanently stuck face down in mud. And yet within min-utes it was pulled up to its near former glory, with a little help from its Tonka truck friends.

Bernie moved to touch my arm and pointed toward the tractor operator. "Becky, that is Curt Bitterman. His brother was Chet Bitterman. You may remember the young missionary, husband, and father who was kidnapped in 1982?"

Did I ever. Along with everyone else I knew, I had watched the news as the world held its collective breath in prayer during Chet's final days.

"Oh, Bernie," I said with emotion, "I'll never forget when the news came in that Chet had been shot in the head by his Colombian captors. I was standing in line in the grocery store. There was not a dry eye in sight."

As Bernie shared more, I realized Curt had fully experienced the results of man's cruelty. Of course he'd struggled with the seemingly senseless waste of life. And yet this was Curt's twenty-fifth year to come back to this place, driving down from Pennsylvania, to volunteer his vacation to work with a camp full of dirty, sweat-soaked, enthusiastic teenagers.

Resiliency. Determination. Curt and his family had made a conscious choice to not allow tragedy to dig ditches of hate in their minds. They would live out their days with generosity and love, in a way that would honor Chet's life.

I glanced at my watch and realized it was nearly time for my big talk under the Big Top. But before I took my leave, a tiny diapered girl with soft blond curls ran over to Bernie's embrace. "This is Jessica," Bernie said, beaming with pride. "She's one of the leader's daughters. Isn't she precious?"

Jessica nuzzled Bernie's arm and smiled at me coyly. "Bob-Bob!" She was suddenly alive with motion, having spotted Bob on a tractor below us. "Bob-Bob!" Jessica's dimpled hands stretched out in his direction. *Those Bland guys are quite the babe magnets*, I thought with a grin.

Half an hour later I was sitting under the huge red-and-white tent waiting my turn to speak. With the singing of each familiar chorus, warm waves of nostalgia washed over me. I remembered, oh so clearly now, how it felt to be on the verge of a youthful quest, fired up with a passion for the Lord. I was fifteen again, at least in my head.

Bob sprinted to the platform, as easily as he did back when I was a kid and he was—well, the age I am now. The teams, though exhausted and filthy from two weeks of training and working, still had plenty of shoutin' energy, which they used to cheer Bob on stage.

Bob's presence was electric, as always, his voice deep and steady and calm. It takes a special man to corral 1,500 hormone-filled, adrenaline-charged teenagers, much less to inspire them to give up TV, air-conditioning, and ice cubes for weeks of intensive training and serving. I've seen youth ministers struggle to control small groups of kids, yet here was a seventy-year-old man with more than a thousand kids hanging on his every word.

This particular night, the teams had been treated to a half-mile-long taco and a 500-gallon milk shake, so they were in especially high spirits. The making of the milk shake had been quite the affair. Curt Bitterman, dressed in an astronaut suit, was lowered into a huge stainless steel vat to mix up the chocolate syrup, milk, and ice cream with a trolling motor. (Men and their ever-lovin' machines!) And yes, of course, this was Bob's innovative idea, a way to congratulate the kids for surviving thus far.

I wondered if these teenagers realized that behind Bob Bland's powerful personality stands a quiet, diminutive wife who applauds his efforts, challenges him when he is wrong, prays for him constantly, loves him unconditionally, and joins him in body and spirit wherever he goes, whether it is to start a new orphanage or to cheer as he pulls tractors from mud.

I had once asked Bernie, "Where was your favorite place in the world to take a team?"

"I'd have to say Papua New Guinea. It was the most isolated

location. Absolutely nothing out there—no stores, no conveniences." Here she paused, grinned, and with a soft hint of mischief added, "I like taking kids to the most remote places. It's more challenging that way, and I love a challenge."

"Does Bob ever go on his overseas trips alone?"

"Oh, no. I won't let him go alone," she had answered, wrinkling her brow. "He needs me too much."

I smiled and nodded. "Your marriage is special, isn't it?"

"Oh, yes, I think so," she replied. "Of course Bob won't even count the first two years we were married because they were so awful. But we adjusted, and have always turned toward each other for comfort."

I loved that phrase: *turning toward each other*. For nearly half a century Bob and Bernie have held each other through countless prayers and bottomless days. They've been poor and sick and grief-stricken—they've cashed in all the downsides of the wedding vows. And yet . . .

They are also rich

and well

and joyous.

How can that be? Then I realized I already knew the answer, for I could hear Bob's echo across the years, "When the going gets tough, the tough get going."

There are too many precious children in want of the Savior's love—from AIDS orphans in Africa, to adorable toddlers, to teenagers with big hopes, huge questions, and no experience. Too many needs to linger long at the well of tears.

So while grief still grips the Bland family, life will go forward. Love still goes on. Bob will mount his bike and peddle off to fix the next leaky pipe or calm the next complaint. Bernie will hobble out to plan a camp-wide meal or mend a homesick heart. The hope of the future—clad in dirty overalls and muddy boots—awaits them.

And I am convinced that a handsome hunk of a grandson, dark eyes glistening with eternal joy, is cheering them from heaven's sidelines . . .

With a smile as big as Christmas morning.[2]

Joel Bland

On Courage

"Often the test of courage is not to die but to live."[3]
—*Vittorio Alfieri*

"God's comfort doesn't walk on tiptoe as in a sick-room; it marches. There is steel in its backbone.

It makes us remember that the word *comfort* is derived from the word *fortis*—which means strong."[4]

At moments when the future is completely obscured, I thought, can any one of us afford to go to meet our tomorrow's with dragging feet? God had been in the past. Then He would be in the future, too.

And with His presence had always come an end to tasteless living. Always he had brought adventure—high hopes, unexpected friends, new ventures that broke old patterns. Then out in my future must lie more goodness, more mercy, more adventures, more friends.

Across the hills light was breaking through the storm clouds. Suddenly just ahead of the car an iridescent rainbow appeared—hung there—shimmering. I hadn't seen a rainbow for a long time.

I drove steadily into the light.[5]
—*From To Live Again, by Catherine Marshall*

Part 3

Magnolias Floating from the Family Tree

*What mother in the world would not
only allow this, but enjoy it?*
—My mother, speaking of Nonnie, my grandmother

Nonnie, Ruthie (Becky's mom), Becky, and daughter Rachel in 1988.

14

Crepe Myrtle Memories

*F*rom the time I was old enough to say "Y'all come," my mother and my aunts, whom I held in high regard, taught me the four lessons of being a true Southern lady, more often by example than by instruction:

1. Be gracious at all times. As the Southern-bred grandmother said to her grown daughter in the film *Hope Floats,* "This family may be strange, but we are NEVER rude."

2. Do the best with the outside the good Lord gave you. I have wonderful, cozy, morning-time memories of watching my aunts and my mother applying their makeup in near-sacramental order: moisturizer, base, eye makeup, eyelash curler, rouge, lipstick, powder over face, powder over lipstick, lipstick again, and—with ceremonial flair—the famous Lipstick and Tissue Blot. All this was followed by a ritual announcement, delivered with plenty of ham and a generous dollop of honey: "Any old barn looks better with a coat of paint."

3. Part of being a beautiful woman is learning to have a good laugh at yourself. Family reunions were virtual storytelling fests as one by one, aunts, uncles, and cousins told the funniest or most embarrassing thing that happened to themselves each year.

As a result, I happily survived many moments that would mortify most teenagers. To me, it was all material for the reunion, which brings me to lesson four.

4. *When given a choice between simple recitation of facts and theatrical delivery, always lean toward drama.* I'd have preferred to listen to Aunt Etta, Aunt Martha, Aunt Deon, and Aunt Velma, along with my mother, cutting up and gossiping around my Nonnie's yellow Formica table, than to attend any play or movie. I can still smell the hot coffee brewing in the tall electric chrome pot; see our quiet Nonnie, ever-aproned and stirring at something on the old gas stove; hear the hilarity pouring from that special company of women, known around Sweetwater, Texas, as, simply, The Jones Girls, as they retold their most entertaining mishaps in spellbinding detail.

For better or worse, for richer for poorer, in sickness and in health, decade upon decade, the laughter still lingers in kitchens of the family at large—over tables of Formica in newlywed apartments, antique oak surfaces in traditional homes, glass and marble counters in downtown condos.

My grandmother, Nonnie, reared her family in a conservative West Texas church, and though her kindness and self-sacrifice endeared her to each of her seven children (and their children and their children . . .) each made their own way. Some chose paths Nonnie would have blessed and amened, and some chose ways that would have worried her to the point of saying, "Well. . . now . . . Hon, I just don't know if that's *best* . . ."

Some of my relatives stayed in the conservative denomination of their childhood; some (like my immediate family) embraced the central gospel of Christ but fellowship in a variety of churches; some commune with God on the fishing lake at sunrise. Some—especially those who hit young adulthood in the era of the sixties—have sought peace and purpose in Eastern philosophies.

Our family's history, like most, is peppered with grace and

grudges, brilliancy and eccentricity, laughter and love, and heart-wrenching grief. Those in our family's tree, with its deeply religious roots, discovered—sometimes in shock—that bad things can and do, indeed, happen to good people.

In the '50s my Uncle Joe—whom I deeply regret not having ever known—fell from a rooftop, lingering in an iron lung before finally widowing his young wife and breaking Nonnie's heart by leaving her so soon. My Uncle Lloyd was injured in a near-fatal auto crash—the afternoon of Uncle Genie and Aunt Deon's wedding day. My parent's first baby girl, who would have been my big sister, was perfectly formed but stillborn, a result of sudden late-term toxemia.

The second generation has also had their portions of grief to bear. AIDS took the life of a beloved cousin. As we grew up, we found, as I suppose all families eventually do, that we are not immune to the devastation of divorce and alcoholism and joblessness and eating disorders, or illness and accidents. And yet—there is laughter in the midst of the pain; there is prayer in the still of the night; there is hope in the restoration of relationships once thought beyond repair.

In a word, there is *family love*. And as much as our families fail us at times, as distant as we ofttimes grow, there are roots that connect us in ways beyond reason.

One of those roots—perhaps the most obvious to our expanding clan—is the precious memory of one special Magnolia, our Nonnie. (If the Lord allows aprons over the gowns of celestial garb, she should be easy to spot in heaven.) I can't wait to be held in her arms again, arms that were always tanned from the sunny hours she spent pruning her crepe myrtles and tending her flowers. How well I remember the comforting feeling of being cushioned against her grandmotherly bosoms, perfect twin pillows for a drowsy grandchild.

Aunt Etta, the oldest female of Nonnie's children, was the first writer in our family. Once she met with publishing success, she encouraged her little sister, my mother—the only other girl in the family—to write professionally. Within a couple of decades my mother, in turn, introduced me to the ecstasy of writing and the agony of rejection letters.

Now I am passing on the family writing torch to yet another Magnolia in our family tree. For my sister Rachel has now joined our writing ranks, creating humorous articles and unique travel pieces for publications such as *Better Homes and Gardens*. I can't help but wonder who will be the next writer to bud and blossom? My daughter? A son? A grandchild perhaps?

I don't know. I only pray there will always be someone in our family willing to be the Keeper of the Stories. It is in the wrapping of a good story that vital lessons are passed down, remembered from one generation to the next. For no one, after all, is story-deaf.

And now I want to invite you to "come on in" to our memories of an old graying house on East Broadway Street in Sweetwater, Texas, and meet Nonnie, the matriarchal Magnolia of the Jones family, through the eyes of her daughters—my writing mentors.

Plum Blossoms in Her Hair
by Etta Lynch, Mom's oldest sister

Nonnie and I lived through The Great Depression surrounded by men—my father and five brothers. I was the only girl until my little sister Ruthie was born, the year I turned thirteen. It was expected that the oldest daughter would don an apron and help Nonnie in the kitchen, so of course, I did. A meal for eight always presented a major problem, since everyone in our small town was poor and my father adamantly refused to "go on relief."

I watched my mother make a breakfast for eight out of cornmeal poured into boiling water. Mush. Mush was good with syrup—if you had any. If not, you stirred sugar into it, and if you were lucky enough to have spices, cinnamon. I watched her save any leftover mush to fry for the evening meal.

She made gravy by beating lard, adding flour, and instead of milk, which we rarely had, she used water. Then, she made water biscuits, with lard, water, flour, salt, and a wee bit of sugar. I never saw her throw one biscuit away. "They'll be good split and toasted in the oven tonight," she reminded.

So, I learned frugality. Today, my grown daughter watches me repeat these thrifty techniques in my kitchen, although there is no need. My living is adequate, if not bountiful. "Mother," she says, "if we ever hit another depression, I need to come home for a week and learn how to live frugally." And I smile. "Better make that a month, Joy." Because frugality is a loooooooonnnnnggg process, and it hurts at times.

However, let me assure you that these times were not as unhappy and miserable as they sound. Nonnie worked hard to make them not only bearable but fun. She dreaded the long, hard, bitterly cold winters because she was extremely cold-natured, and our wood-burning stove warmed only one room: the kitchen. I helped her drag an old Singer sewing machine into the kitchen, and she made my bloomers from flour sacks. I lived in horror of falling off the seesaw at school, for fear someone would see the bright letters across my bottom: Gladiola Flour.

One day Nonnie stripped the last strand off a spool of thread and tucked the spool back into a machine drawer. "Mother, let me throw that in the trash," I said. She shook her head. "No. There'll be a use for it someday."

For an empty spool? I wondered if she was "slipping a cog," as we said in those days. Then, winter came. Icy winds and snow kept us inside for days, sometimes missing school because the school buses couldn't run. Nonnie called us to the warm kitchen. "You kids sit down in a circle." We did, wondering. She put a bowl in the center of our circle, containing chunks of homemade lye soap and a little water.

From her apron pocket she took six of those spools I thought she should have discarded and handed one to each of us. She took her spool, rubbed it across the lye soap, and then dipped it into the water. To our amazement, she blew a huge bubble that lingered at the end her spool until she jerked it sideways. The bubble broke loose and floated around the room, reflecting the rays of the kerosene lamp and our own amazed images.

To us, this was absolute magic, and we spent hours experimenting to see who could blow the biggest bubble or the bubble that would last longest. In spite of our enjoyment, we sometimes forgot and tilted our heads back while blowing. That lye soap tasted simply horrible!

When spring came we all felt great relief and when school was out, the older ones roamed the nearby sandhills. One late afternoon, three of us walked through a plum thicket near our house; the bushes were covered with beautiful white blooms. One of my brothers, Lloyd, picked a cluster and carried it to the house.

In the kitchen Nonnie was stirring a pot of soup and making cornbread, but she looked up and smiled. "Have a good time?"

Lloyd approached her from behind, tucked the cluster of plum blossoms in her hair, and whirled her around. "One, two, three . . . waltz! Way down in Missouri, where I heard this melody . . ." Strong and taller than she, he maneuvered her around the kitchen table. By then, we had all caught his spirit and began clapping and singing with him.

Nonnie strongly disapproved of dancing, but her innate

sense of humor got the best of her, and she began to giggle. We all joined in, and the laughter reached the uncontrollable point. Nonnie dropped into a chair, breathless and laughing so hard tears ran down her cheeks. She wiped them away with her apron and we all rushed to hug and congratulate her. For what? For being a part of the fun. For being a wonderful sport, in spite of her strict beliefs.

Many years later I married and returned to Sweetwater for Thanksgiving. As always, I arrived the night before to help prepare the turkey, cook cornbread for the dressing, etc. Nonnie and I enjoyed a warm mother-oldest daughter time planning for the next day's avalanche of my siblings, their children, my children, and grandchildren.

The Thanksgiving dinner was perfect—a huge turkey, browned and succulent. Dressing that melted in your mouth. Cranberry sauce, fruit salad, and desserts that were so rich they were almost immoral. I thought of those Spartan days during the Depression and thanked the good Lord that our mother no longer was forced to scrimp, to make water gravy and mush.

I carried dishes to the kitchen and noticed a spot on the floor. Bending over it, I examined it closely. Dressing? Someone had dropped it and someone else had stepped in it. Disgusting! "What on earth is this?" I asked.

Nonnie, who was close behind me, leaned over my shoulder. "Whatever it is, save it."

I collapsed with laughter and the others filed in one by one. My family cannot bear to hear chuckling and chortling and not know the reason. When I told them, the house simply rang with laughter.

To this day, we share this story with new members of the family, and it will be passed on and on and on and . . .

If only she could be here to share the fun that we talk about, relive, and will always cherish.

A Sweet Gardenia of Endurance
by Ruthie Arnold, my mother

Life is very rarely all ease or all struggle, and pity the human being who, in either condition, cannot find plenty to laugh about.

Looking back, I see my life at home as a kaleidoscope of mixed emotions, much of the time. I remember Mother's quiet tears and my father's noisy anger; I remember my preschool years during a sober time in Daddy's life when he told me wonderful stories in the evening, and let me comb his wavy auburn hair, and sometimes carried me on his shoulders. As a four- and five-year-old child, I had no idea that, long before I was born, he had struggled with alcoholism.

Even so, after my father began to drink again, we kiddos still found ways and times to have lots of fun. Sometimes he went off to town, and we didn't have to be so quiet and careful. Other times he was away for long periods in the veteran's hospital, sobering up and trying to get his life together, which took many tries before, late in life, he finally succeeded.

Sometimes, Daddy even worked! This was great cause for celebration, but most of his time he spent closed away from the family in his bedroom, reading or sleeping. We would have our meals with Mother, gathered around the old wooden table, talking and laughing and having a marvelous time. (By this time, we were all contributing to the grocery bill, so the food was wonderful: Mother's fried chicken and steak, heaping bowls of mashed potatoes and cream gravy, 'nanner puddin' . . .)

A big part of what I remember are the antics of five big

brothers, playing tricks on each other, and how much fun it was to watch them. And then suddenly, suddenly, they were all gone, and I was alone.

I missed them, but how I enjoyed having Mother all to myself. That's one of the blessings of being the youngest in a big family.

I worked in a department store through high school and loved being able to buy Mother a few small gifts now and then with my employee's discount. We did not have a family car, so I walked everywhere I went—a mile to high school unless friends came by for me, and a mile or more to work at midday from high school, and then in the evening after work, two miles home.

Daddy was sober by then, and though I was still so angry I would not speak to him, he was working and making enough money to pay the bills, so Mother's stress was greatly reduced.

It was so quiet in the big old house that had rung with laughter and activity, and occasionally, with shouts of anger. And then my brother, James, came home from Korea. And James had a car! Thus begins one of the happiest times I remember being at home.

This handsome big brother seemed proud of his budding little teenage sister, and chauffeured me almost anywhere I wanted to go. He drove me home after my workday and even picked me up at school at lunchtime, bringing me to a wonderful noon meal prepared of course, by Nonnie. Since all his buddies were gone away to war or to college, he was lonesome enough to squire me around, and we spent many pleasant hours in a booth at Mrs. Starr's restaurant, having coffee and talking. And then he happened to notice my best friend, Martha.

Martha was tall and willowy, a brunette beauty. The boys in our school who had not yet gotten their full growth, didn't quite know what they were missing. James, a good six feet tall, almost drove up a lamp post in downtown Sweetwater when he spotted Martha walking down the street. And to my great joy, they began to date. This meant that most of the time when James picked me up at noon for lunch, Martha came along too. Let me tell you, there's just nothing any more fun than having your big brother date your best friend.

I will always remember the day Martha and I reached across Nonnie's table at the same time for the same fried chicken breast. We each connected with the chicken, and our eyes locked across the table, each grinning a wicked grin. I pulled, she pulled, James started to chuckle, and Nonnie began to laugh and to sputter at the same time. "Now, girls . . ."

Martha was taller than I was, so I stood up to get a little more traction under my feet, keeping a firm grip on the chicken. I pulled again, but no luck. Martha rose to her feet, and laughing, we began to maneuver around the table, the chicken between us.

By this time, James and Mother were just trying to avoid getting grease and gravy all over them, since once Martha and I reached the front hallway, we had grease up to our elbows. The problem now became not only to hold onto the slick chicken, but not to lose our strength—as we were almost too tickled to stand. As I recall, we resolved the issue by sitting down in the floor together, each still firmly gripping the chicken breast, and taking turns with bites.

Nonnie laughed and laughed, wiping her eyes on her apron and shaking her head. I knew it was an outrageous antic, and somewhere inside I remember thinking, What mother in the world would not only allow this, but enjoy it?

And I knew, as I often knew in such happy moments, that this was a wonderful mother, and we were blessed with *joy. I felt, all the way through to graduation, and even with my unresolved anger against my dad, that I was very close to having a normal teenage life—the extra love and laughter in our kitchen, somehow balancing the emotional scales.*

I often talk about my mother as being a woman of tremendous strength, and that she was. But her strength was to endure, not to fight. In my junior high years, when several of us young'uns were still at home, I recall doing my best to persuade her to leave Daddy.

"Where would we go? What would we live on?" was usually her first line of defense.

"What would we live on?!" I would roar. "We kids are supporting him!" (If you ask my family what one adjective they would have chosen to describe me in my growing-up years, it would probably be "feisty.")

Then she would get to the crux of the matter. "Honey," she would counter, "the Bible says, 'let the unbelieving one depart.' And I believe adultery is the only biblical reason for divorce. Your daddy has never been unfaithful."

As I write this today, I know Nonnie's words may sound archaic to some. And I'm not sure her interpretation of this scripture is completely accurate, or if I, in her position, could have stayed with a man like my father. At any rate, this verse was one of the things that held her to him.

Many years later Mother and I sat together in the yellow kitchen, and I plied her with questions arising out of mid-life, when answers are not quite as plentiful and obvious as they'd seemed in my youth.

"Do you ever regret not leaving Daddy and trying to make a different life for yourself?" I asked.

"What would he have done without me?" she asked softly. " What would have become of him?" She smoothed the paper napkin in front of her with her veined and arthritic hands, thinking. "No," she decided firmly, "I don't

regret staying with him. I would have missed the years after he stopped drinking, and we had a little more money and he was a lot easier to live with. We had some good times, Ruthie. Those would have been lonely years, especially after all you kiddos left."

Yes, and I had had some good times with him too. Some healing times that have meant so much to me as an adult. Would those times have been possible if she had left him as I'd once wanted her to do? This Real Magnolia of a mama taught me one of many crucial lessons: marriage is meant to be forever, and for reasons we may not see in the middle of our pain.

Another time I remember asking my mother, "Do you ever get to the point that you don't fret about your children?" She was seventy-six at the time, and I was looking for a time when my worries might come to an end.

"No, Honey," she said ruefully. "You never do."

It was one of those good news/bad news deals. Some of my joy would always be affected by how my kids were faring, but at the same time, I was glad to know at age forty-three, my mother still cared deeply about what happened to me and mine, and would never stop praying for me.

Not only did we kids love our mother, she was embraced as a mother figure by many others in our small town, everyone calling her "Nonnie." I remember when I was about eleven years old I had earned babysitting money to buy Mother a corsage, and I chose a gardenia. I thought it was absolutely gorgeous and was so excited about how thrilled she would be. Imagine my chagrin when that Saturday afternoon, a series of florist trucks pulled up in front of our old house until there were FOUR orchid corsages in Nonnie's refrigerator for Sunday morning. One from the insurance man, one from a young man whose mother had died when he was young, one from a family for *whom Nonnie was a surrogate grandmother—and one from a brother. She wore one corsage Sunday morning, one Sunday evening, and saved the other two for the following Sunday.*

After that, the six of us kids conferred to be sure who was sending a flower, because we all wanted to be sure she had at least one. Usually it was an orchid, but she and I always had a secret joke between us: We really liked gardenias best!

Peter Stillman, in his book, *Families Writing*, said, "The richer a family is in stories, the greater the legacy to pass on." How thankful I am for the window of my mother's and Aunt Etta's stories, opening curtains for generations to come, so they, too, might catch a glimpse of the lady who offered red beans and cornbread, and cups filled with kindness to all who graced her kitchen table. A woman named Elsie Pearl Jones, better known as simply our "Nonnie."

Do not think me fanciful
  too imaginative
    or too extravagant in my language
when I say that I think of women, and particularly
of our mothers, as Keepers of the Springs. The
phrase, while poetic, is true and descriptive.
  We feel its warmth . . .
    its softening influence . . .
      and however forgetful we have been . . .
however much we have taken for granted life's
precious gifts
we are conscious of wistful memories that surge
out of the past—
  the sweet
    tender
      poignant fragrances of love.
    . . . So I shall make my tribute a plea for
Keepers of the Springs, who will be faithful to their
tasks.[1]

—Peter Marshall

When the mind says, "It's possible!" the body and spirit unite in a supreme effort to prove it.
—Etta Lynch, Mom's sister and my amazing aunt

Jimmy and Etta Lynch

15

Waltzin' Magnolia

When I think back on memories of my Aunt Etta, I can't help thinking of her husband, my Uncle Jimmy. Then, I think of dancing.

I especially think of one memorable, uproarious night—the night we had a hoedown in my parents' living room. I can almost see the furniture pushed back against the wall, hear the country harmonies beckoning us to move our feet in rhythm. Talk about pure, unadulterated fun! All evening long, Aunt Etta and Uncle Jimmy taught the lot of us (Mother and Daddy, Scott and me, and my two siblings) to schottische, two-step, polka, waltz—and do a line dance to an old tune called "Pinto Beans." We were a house full of dancin' fools, with Jimmy and Etta serving as the "Fred and Ginger" of the family room.

So stunning were Etta and Jimmy when they stepped on an actual dance floor, that folks couldn't help pausing with wistful wonder, backing up as the elegant couple waltzed by, dipping and turning with effortless grace. They moved fluidly, effortlessly, like a pair of swans over a lake of glass.

Aunt Etta was tall and ever resplendent. Her cheekbones regal, her smile wide and lovely, her auburn hair always done up in a perfect French twist. She had a figure to rival any twenty-year-old, and legs—oh, those legs: long, and lean and incredibly lovely. She always wore a slim, tailored dress, or sometimes a skirt and fitted blouse, with hose and strappy high heels. This was her standard attire, even to the grocery store or a neighbor's backyard barbeque. (Much to the gratitude of any gentlemen blessed with a view, I imagine.)

Uncle Jimmy was equally striking. He was six feet tall, solid as the steel trains he engineered down the tracks. Above his ruggedly handsome face, his jet black hair was always combed straight back. (Until his graying hair began to thin and Etta gave him permanents.) His mustache was thick and dark as coal. (When Etta and Jimmy went to Mexico as tourists, the natives eased into their native tongue around Jimmy, assuming he was one of them. Ironically, the fair-skinned Etta was the one who spoke flawless Spanish.) He looked exotic, mysterious, even a bit dangerous—though I was never afraid of him. He was always kind to me with a ready sense of humor.

For the most part, Jimmy and Etta lived their lives the same way they danced: together. Their daily routines of breakfasting late, watching the news, and dancing three nights a week, were as much in sync as their two-step. Though Etta loved Jimmy fiercely, she sometimes longed for more breathing room in their marriage. He was not big on socializing, other than chatting and dancing with her. Etta had many passions: friends, cooking, writing, teaching. When Jimmy retired from the railroad, he had one passion: Etta. At times this felt like an honor, at other times a burden. (As the saying goes, "I married my husband for life, but not for lunch!")

Last year, after an extended period of heart problems, Uncle Jimmy passed away at age eighty. Though Etta grieved his loss, she did not sit and whittle away.

It is impossible, actually, for me to imagine anything that would knock Aunt Etta off her feet. Those graceful, lovely legs, even at age seventy-four, are sturdy and strong, taking her forward one step at a time to the future. She has discovered a whole new dance: a solo ballet with life, one full of grace with some surprising turns.

This summer, a brown package came in the morning's mail. Inside was a book and a newspaper clipping from Lubbock, Texas (where Aunt Etta has lived for forty-two years), dated June 1998. I grabbed the manila envelope, along with a pair of sunglasses and a glass of iced tea, and headed down to the dock to savor its contents.

Lubbock writer Etta Lynch keeps getting requests for her book Help is Only a Prayer Away, *published by Fleming H. Revell in the early 1970s. The problem is, the book sold out and the publisher chose not to reprint . . .*

As people have continued to call her and ask for copies, she has decided to print 1,000 copies.

"Already I have orders coming in for ten and twenty copies at a time," she said, "but my problem is, I'm attending classes at St. Edward's University in Austin, getting a degree."

At seventy-four, she drives eight hours to get to Austin for class and drives back the next day to teach creative writing in the continuing education department at Texas Tech. Therefore, time for marketing her reprinting of the book is limited, she said.

The inspirational stories are timeless. In the second chapter, titled "Death Slept Between Us," she tells her personal story of her husband's battle with cancer . . ."

The article went on to describe the book and to name Etta's various award-winning works, including a short story that was made into a movie, "A Different Drum," the first all-Native American movie ever produced. I inwardly applauded my feisty aunt, getting her degree in the middle of her seventh decade of life—and driving 8 hours, one way, to do it!

How well I remember when *Help is Only a Prayer Away* first came out. I was thirteen, and told everybody at school I was related to a famous author. When we were assigned to write a report about a well-known figure in history, I wrote about my Aunt Etta, the *great author*. The whole family drove out to Sweetwater, Texas, to attend Etta's first booksigning. I got to go along, standing at Etta's side as she signed copies and introduced me to her hometown friends. I may as well have been asked to accompany the Queen of England to her coronation ball.

The newspaper's mention of the story, "Death Slept Between Us," brought with it another fresh batch of memories. As a child I'd only known Uncle Jimmy as a strapping man, who could lift me off the ground with one sweep of his muscled arm. Hard to believe there had been a time when he was too weak to walk, much less pick up a small child, a time when his life hung in the fragile gap between earth and heaven.

I reached into the brown envelope and pulled out my autographed copy of *Help is Only a Prayer Away*, held it to my chest for a moment, then began to read the old family story again, for the first time in twenty-six years.

Death Slept Between Us
by Etta Lynch

(excerpted from *Help is Only a Prayer Away,* 1972, reprinted 1998)

For five years a feared and hated guest forced his presence in our home. He ate every meal with us, took vacations with us and slept between us at night. Unexpected and uninvited, he moved in Sunday afternoon, April 17, 1961. His name was Death.

My husband, Jimmy, in his late forties, took off his shirt and went outside to mow his dad's small scraggly lawn.

His father had a recent cataract operation and couldn't exert himself in any way. We sat on the front porch watching Jimmy and giving good-natured advice. Jimmy's straight black hair fell forward on his forehead, and his muscles rippled under the smooth, tanned skin. My husband was an extremely handsome man.

Suddenly he stopped mowing, turned toward me, and the color drained from his face. He reeled slightly, grabbing the lawn mower for support. It moved forward and he almost fell.

"What's the matter, Jimmy?" I jumped off the porch and ran to him frantically.

"Help me," he said, thickly, throwing an arm across my shoulders, his 200 pounds almost buckling my knees. His skin sickened with cold, clammy perspiration and the muscles in his legs jerked uncontrollably. His father hurried to the other side. Leaning on us heavily, Jimmy staggered into the house and collapsed on the divan. Panic-stricken, I put a cold wet cloth on his forehead.

"Mom," I fought to steady my voice. "Call an ambulance. Jimmy's having a heart attack."

"No!" Jimmy grabbed my arm and struggled to sit up, trying to be forceful, but his voice came out a weak gasp. "My heart doesn't hurt. Nothing hurts. I just feel like I'm going to die. I'm so weak I don't feel like I'd weigh fifty pounds."

I studied him with alarm. If anything happened to him, life wouldn't be worth living for me. "Let me call a doctor, Jimmy, please."

"Just give me a second," he said, lying back again. "I'll be all right."

I put my fingers on his pulse, watching his face anxiously. His pulse raced, thready and uneven.

After a few minutes he took a long ragged breath and sat up, blinking as though he'd awakened from a nightmare. "I don't feel so weak anymore. I'm going to finish mowing that lawn if it kills me."

In spite of our protests, he went out to master the rest of that lawn. I watched him, almost in tears, admiring his tenacity but worried sick. We'd found each other late in life. Jimmy was forty-four years old; I was thirty-six. We'd been married only five years and I'd never known happiness like ours existed. Mowing that lawn was the last act of physical labor Jimmy performed for five months.

That afternoon we drove back to Lubbock and Jimmy went straight to bed. The next morning his legs were weak, and he had a temperature. He called the railroad and told them to call another engineer for his shift. Without asking him, I phoned our doctor. Jimmy was insulted, but I think he was secretly relieved.

He insisted on going to the doctor alone, and I vacuumed the living room carpet to pass the time. It didn't need cleaning, but I could see the driveway from that room. Too, the roar of the vacuum helped me shut out the awful things I imagined the doctor might be telling Jimmy.

At five o'clock the car swung into the drive and I switched the vacuum off, searching his face as he walked up the sidewalk. Under their heavy black brows, his eyes had the stunned look of a man who had been hit a blow in the back of the head. Something was wrong, very wrong. The certainty pierced me like a sliver of ice next to my heart. Rushing to the door, I grabbed him by both arms.

"What is it?" I commanded insistently, my fingernails digging in. "What's the matter?"

"Nothing's the matter, Goofy." He smiled, but it didn't reach his eyes. "You're digging holes in my arms. Cut it out."

His voice rasped, strained and unnatural. I loved him too much for him to be able to cover up when he suffered this badly. He was lying to ease my pain.

"Jimmy, we've never lied to each other. Let's not start now."

He reached out and pulled me into his arms, buried his face in my neck and held me as if he would never let me go.

"I'm a goner," he admitted, his voice muffled against my neck.

My arms tightened around him and a premonition of disaster lanced though me. "What do you mean?" I whispered.

"Cancer."

Somewhere inside me a wall disintegrated, releasing the hurting tears. We held each other and cried bitterly.

Finally I raised my head. "Maybe the doctor is mistaken."

"There's no mistake." Jimmy blew his nose and composed his face. "He's so sure, he booked me for surgery in the morning at Temple Hospital. A surgeon from Scott and White will do it."

"And you weren't going to tell me?" I asked incredulously.

"About the surgery, yes; but not the cancer."

I dropped into a chair, my knees too weak to support me. I tried the word in my mind. Cancer. A simple word—six letters. Bad applied to anyone, but applied to my husband, it brought cold sweat all over my body, and I knew the brassy taste of abject fear. I'd heard of too many who had operations and never got out of the hospital. He looked too well for the malignancy to be advanced. I couldn't say anything, but I hoped desperately he'd decide against surgery. At least I'd have him whole for a while.

"Are you going?" I managed finally.

"I guess so." He swallowed hard. "We have to do something. We can't just sit here."

We left that same night at nine o'clock. Driving into Temple at three A.M., we found the old Santa Fe Railroad Hospital and nosed into a parking place. Lights from the upper wing slanted across a magnolia tree beside the hospital entrance, spotlighting huge white blooms against waxy dark green leaves. So beautiful and perfect! Surely a Creator who had made something this lovely would be interested in one of His creatures.

"Maybe," I began hesitantly, turning toward Jimmy, "maybe we ought to pray."

In answer he took my hand and bowed his head silently. Jimmy had never believed in public prayer, so no formal pattern of prayer came to my stricken mind, only the plea, Let him live. Let him live. Please, God, let him live. The silence pulsed beneath our unspoken petitions and after a few moments Jimmy raised his head, leaned over, and kissed me. We held hands and talked until darkness changed to ever lighter shades of gray, and I felt a sense of surprise that the sun could come up as normally as if nothing had happened.

Twice before in my life I'd prayed that someone I loved be spared, and my prayer had gone no higher than the ceiling. I remembered sitting beside my younger brother in an iron lung, praying God would spare his life and return him to our family. He lived five days. I'd prayed for an uncle I loved like a father. He'd taught me to love books and to know I could do anything if I worked hard enough. I'd prayed for his life and God had closed His ears. And now Jimmy. I felt as if I would fly into a thousand pieces.

Later that day they wheeled him out of surgery. He was still under anesthesia but moaning softly. The doctor followed, his mask still hanging around his neck, and motioned me to a chair.

"There's no doubt in my mind that this growth is malignant, but I'm sure we got it all. We removed the left testicle and the cord. This should keep it from spreading through the lymph system. He stood the operation fine." Getting to his feet, he smiled down at me. "Try not to worry. We'll hit this with X-ray therapy to be on the safe side, but this is just a precaution."

I hurried into Jimmy's room and leaned over him. He moistened his lips. "Was it . . .?"

"Yes, it was, but they got it all." I took his hand and held it in both my own against my breast. "You're going to be fine."

Two days later a nurse called me out of Jimmy's hospital room and ushered me into an office where six doctors waited. Sensing disaster, my fear antennae went up. If the news was good, only one doctor would need to tell me. I sank into a chair, clutching my purse and my composure with both hands.

"Mrs. Lynch," one of the doctors said, clearing his throat and speaking cautiously, "Because the malignancy is in this particular part of your husband's body, it's extremely difficult to keep it confined to that area."

My befuddled layman's mind recorded his words and tried to make sense of them. "You mean . . . it's spread already?"

I looked at the doctors, who all returned my gaze steadily. This had to be one of those dreams, when you realize you're asleep, yet the horror is so vivid it almost crushes you.

"Is . . . is there any hope?" I stammered.

As if all their heads were manipulated by the same string, the six doctors shook their heads. "I'd say six months to two years, at most," one said gently.

Blankly I stared at them but saw nothing. The long vista of a future without Jimmy stretched before me, desolate and bleak. Tears slid down my cheeks and dropped on my dress front, splotching it darkly. So this was God's answer to our prayer. I got to my feet and left the room, tired and aching in every joint. I felt old beyond belief.

The rambling old Santa Fe Hospital became our home.

Sometimes we ate in the dining hall with the other patients and their wives; sometimes at a small restaurant across the street. Every day stretched interminably, broken only by the ambulance trip to Scott and White for Jimmy's X-ray treatment, which nauseated him. Twenty pounds melted from his big frame, leaving him gaunt and hollow-eyed.

Suddenly, unbelievably, June arrived and the doctor told Jimmy he could go home. Joyfully, laughing at nothing and everything, we packed his things. Calling good-byes to the patients, we carried his luggage down the hall and stopped at the doctor's office for the eternal red tape of dismissal.

"By the way, Jim." The doctor tapped his stethoscope against Jimmy's chest, emphasizing his words. "You're absolutely not to drive for six weeks."

Jimmy loved cars; the feel of the road beneath a powerful engine was one of his greatest pleasures.

"You've got to be kidding!" my husband exploded, towering over the little doctor as if he would force him to change his mind.

The doctor stood his ground. "You slam the brakes on just one time, and that stomach falls out on the floor." He poked Jimmy very carefully in the midsection. "The X-ray therapy makes the muscles so weak they won't hold. Understand?"

Jimmy nodded, disappointment painting his face. We got the necessary papers, walked slowly to the car, and I got in on the driver's side for the long trip home.

Each year we took a long vacation, covering from three to five thousand miles. This year we'd planned to go to Southern California. If Jimmy gains the strength to take this trip, I thought, he must have a good time. It could so easily be the last.

The day we went through Disneyland, Jimmy's left shoulder began to bother him and the next day his muscles exploded in pain. The thought of his getting sick that far from home panicked me. We drove day and night to get home, going straight to the hospital when we reached Lubbock.

The railroad physician had a thoracic specialist there to meet us.

"Naturally we assume this is a metastasis," he said, his fingers probing the knot at the base of Jimmy's neck.

The news meant the cancer had spread from the site of the original malignancy. It could be the beginning of the end.

"And if it is?" Jimmy's voice shook, then steadied.

"We'll start cobalt treatments as soon as possible."

The next morning the specialist made an incision above the collarbone and found the cancer had spread all through the left side of Jimmy's chest, its tentacles wrapped around the major arteries leading to the heart.

"If I operated, he'd never use his left arm much," he said doubtfully. "All we can do is hit it with cobalt. If you've got to have cancer, he's got the best kind. It's the only type that responds to radiation."

"You mean he might get well?"

"I didn't say that." His tone was gentle. "But it will slow the growth."

"How long?" I almost strangled on the question.

"Six months, maybe." He shrugged, his eyes sad. "We just don't know."

Numbly, I returned to Jimmy's room. Six months, and during that time he must suffer. How could God let this happen?

In the next six weeks, Jimmy absorbed the maximum amount of cobalt. His legs hurt with a deep, bone-piercing ache. The doctors assured us this was the radiation, not cancer of the bone. The skin on Jimmy's neck showed no outer burn, as there had been with the X-ray treatments, but he said it felt exactly like a third-degree burn.

The doctor allowed him to drive, but it exhausted him to drive to the hospital, take his treatment, and get home. He fell on the bed, watched TV, read until his eyes turned fiery red, and then lay there thinking.

All my life I'd been blessed with tremendous physical strength. Going about my housework after a long day working at the beauty shop, I sensed Jimmy's eyes following my movements. He never said anything, but I knew he couldn't help resenting my ability to bend, stoop, and work for hours, when the walk from the bed to the living room left him sick and gasping for breath.

A vast chasm separates the possessor of a healthy body from the one who lives in a damaged, disease-ravaged body, haunted by the certainty of death. I stood on one side of this chasm, and Jimmy stood on the other. Even our great love couldn't bridge the distance. It might as well have been two different worlds. The constraint between us mounted.

A year later a persistent low-grade temperature warned us. And the weakness—always the weakness. This time the tumor showed up in the left lung. He reached his lowest ebb at the hospital when he refused the insult of the bedpan and fell on his way to the bathroom. His head struck the door, and he sported a purple shiner, plus the outraged dignity of the naturally modest man in a too-short nightshirt. Helped back to bed, he refused my sympathy, turning his back.

I took refuge behind the newspaper, hurt and sick. Over and over like a flashing neon sign, my mind relived the sight of Jimmy sprawled unconscious on the cold hospital tile. Now reduced to 170 pounds, Jimmy was too weak to walk even a few feet. An aching compassion for him brought tears to my eyes. Behind that newspaper I prayed earnestly that God would spare him further indignity. If he had to go, let him go proudly, as he had lived.

A feeling of relief overwhelmed me. I felt light-headed, almost floating in my release from dread.

Jimmy rolled over in bed and grinned sheepishly. "You don't have to monopolize the sports page just 'cause I got a black eye."

Eagerly I handed him the sports section of the paper, accepting his gesture of apology with gratitude. "I didn't think you'd feel like reading!"

"I guess that little jolt cleared my head," he said wonderingly. "I feel pretty good."

From that day on, prayer became a constant state for me.

Another six weeks of cobalt, bombarding the left lung. Another vacation with Death hovering in the background, figuring in every decision, dampening our spirits. In San Antonio, Texas, a spasm of coughing racked Jimmy from head to foot. He spit up something that looked exactly like chicken liver.

"Part of my lung . . ." he gasped, his eyes streaming.

He called his doctor long distance and I sat across from him, waiting for the grim verdict. A disbelieving smile lit Jimmy's face, and he hung up quickly.

"It's the tumor! The doctor says it's breaking up!"

I jumped up, grabbed him, and burst into tears. The cobalt might break up the tumor, but too many doctors had agreed he couldn't get well. I wept, not from joy, but out of gratitude that his arms were around me and the constraint between us had disappeared.

Jimmy passed his fifth year, going for checkups every two months at first, and later, every six months.

"I guess you know you're not supposed to be here." The doctor put his X rays back in the folder, his voice betraying his pleasure.

"I didn't really expect to be," Jimmy admitted. "How do you account for it?"

The physician shrugged, looking out the window, his eyes narrowed in thought. "Some imponderable reversal of body chemistry." He grinned, stood, and shook hands with both of us. "Who cares? You're on our cured list. I hope I never see you again . . . professionally."

We left the office hand in hand. Outside the hospital Jimmy stopped, his eyes sweeping the horizon, devouring the trees and greenery. His eyes roved the hospital grounds, touching the people he saw with love and concern. Six doctors had said he couldn't live, yet here he stood, strong again—a living monument to a growing faith.

He looked down at me and something special came into his look, a look meant just for me.

"Imponderable reversal, my foot!" he snorted, smiling broadly. "I won't buy that for a minute. There may be others, but I've never heard of anyone else who had recurrences of cancer three different times, three different places, and lived. It was a reversal all right, but it was God's reversal."

I nodded, unable to speak, but I knew it was so.[1]

I finished the chapter, softly closing the cover of the book, and ran my fingers under the title's bright letters. An involuntary smile formed on my lips.

I confess, I do not know how prayer works. I do not know why God heals some, allows others to linger in pain, and takes others home. I will leave that for the theologians to debate for the next hundred years. Still I do believe God hears our prayers.

As I reread this story, it surprised and warmed me to read that Jimmy and Etta's faith in God's care had been strengenthed, in the lonely dawn hours of a hospital parking lot, by the sight of a magnolia tree with its huge white blooms against waxy dark green leaves. The sight of the tree's flowering beauty caused Etta to muse, "Surely, a Creator who had made something this lovely would be interested in one of His creatures."

After so many years, and in the context of the story's more dramatic scenes, I'd long forgotten this descriptive passage. And now, here I am, an author—writing a book with *magnolias* overflowing its pages. A coincidence, or a heaven-touched message of affirmation?

Even as I write this, chills pebble up my arms. For somehow, in the retelling of this piece of Jimmy and Etta's life, I believe God intended the best and most dazzling of their dances—the one of faith waltzing over the floor of despair—to go on.

Because Aunt Etta is a woman of near mythic proportions in our family tree, I asked my mother, Etta's little sister, to share her own memories of her, in the days before I was born. Though Jimmy and Etta were married for almost forty years, I knew he was not her first husband, nor the biological father of her two children, Joy and Jim Tom (whom I grew up calling T Boy). But I never really knew the story *behind* the story until mother's e-mail came. I found it a fascinating piece to the puzzle of the woman Aunt Etta is today.

Memories of One
Magnificent Magnolia
by Ruthie Arnold

The earliest memory I have of My Big Sister was the day

she came home and threw open the front screen, and stepped in the door with a flourish.

There she stood, her lovely brunette head erect and defiant under a broad-brimmed white hat, her statuesque figure draped in a white jersey dress. The year was 1941. She was sixteen and I was four, but even at four, I knew we were about to have a scene. Nobody in our house ever walked defiantly, except our daddy. Mostly, we walked diffidently.

But Etta was definitely walking defiantly toward my father's bedroom even as I noticed a young man in a sailor's uniform coming up the porch steps just in time to catch the screen door intended to slam behind my sister. I must have followed her into the bedroom because I remember the scene quite clearly.

Our father had been lying down (it was midmorning as I recall) and he sat up on the side of the bed. Maybe he had seen the young sailor waiting in the doorway behind her, but he stayed seated, looking at my sister with narrowed eyes. To me, she seemed to tower over us all, a figure intent with purpose. Hands on her hips, head thrown back under the white hat, she made her statement.

"I told you if you ever whipped me again I'd be married in two weeks. This is my husband. We were married this morning."

Daddy did not move from his seat on the bed, his elbows resting on his knees, his hands dropped between them. He said words to the effect, "Well, Sis, you've done it now," but he said it rather more pungently than that.

If he said anything else, I don't remember, but that must have been the end of the scene because I seem to remember that she introduced her sailor to the rest of the family, and I think she helped fix lunch, which we all ate together. I don't recall how many of her four younger brothers gathered round the table, big-eyed at such goings-on. Daddy had always been the one in charge, but today, we all knew, Etta was in charge. And something big had been settled.

She had made her break. Daddy wouldn't control her again. Ever. And he would never whip her again either.

She must have changed out of her white jersey dress after lunch, because another scene took place that I do not remember, but that has been repeated at every family gathering since 1941. For some reason that afternoon, my brother James was teasing her, and she gave chase, her long legs matching him stride for stride until he must have felt her hot breath on his neck. Deliverance came (he thought) when he leaped over a fence and in a supreme act of reck-lessness, turned to stick his tongue out at Etta, of all people.

Before he could say, "Nya, nya you cain't catch me," she was over the fence and landed right in his middle, married woman or not. To this day, I don't think any of her four younger brothers or one older brother have ever gotten the best of her—not physically and certainly not verbally.

For this was a girl who loved words.

The family still laughs over her statement, at about age eight, that she planned to spend a good deal of her time as an adult lying about on "shif'on" pillows, and eating bonbons.

In high school, she made National Honor Society at the same time she scrubbed houses for the well-to-do in our small town, walking into town to school, then to her work. At the end of the day, she made her way back down the country roads to our house to do what she could to help Mother with her workload. And the money she earned mostly went into Mother's apron pocket to help support our family.

But those days were over now. She had graduated early and with honors, and she had found someone to take her away from her father's heavy hand and the relentless poverty and labor and whippings.

But there was at least one thing Daddy was right about. Sis had really "done it now."

The best that could be said about her marriage was that she had jumped from the fire into the frying pan, and a few short years later, she came back to our house (now in town but not much improved) as a single mother, bringing her three-year-old son and four-year-old daughter.

Typical of Etta, she had laid her plans carefully, going through beauty school so that she would be able to support her children before leaving a marriage that had become impossible for her. And by this time, Daddy was barely functional, drinking heavily. I and two older brothers still needed to get through grade school, junior high, and high school, so Etta opened her shop in downtown Sweetwater to put bread on the table for us all.

Yes, Daddy worked occasionally, but mostly he was more problem than problem solver. We three younger ones also worked as we went through school, earning our own spending money, and Mother took care of Etta's children while she worked. But how many times I remember when I or my brothers needed to make a choir or band trip or to buy a uniform and there was simply no money in Mother's apron pocket. Etta produced it without complaining, even while she produced grocery money at the end of the week to feed all eight of us, and money to keep the lights on and the house warmed.

And then one day a handsome fellow named Jimmy Lynch parked a brand new Buick by our curb, and strolled up the walk to our house, doffing his Stetson hat as he came to call on My Big Sister. Jimmy had wanted to court Etta when she was fourteen and he was twenty-one, but Daddy would have none of it.

Now he was back, still single after all these years, and he wanted to court my sister. After her first disastrous marriage, she was gun shy, as we say in Texas. So Jimmy had to be especially persistent. She had married in haste once, and had repented at leisure. It took Jimmy a long time to convince her that their marriage would be different.

My brother Lloyd had graduated, Gene was almost there, and I was a junior in high school. She figured we could make it without her now. Her own children were preteen, so she packed them up with her and Jimmy and moved to Lubbock where she opened her beauty shop and finished raising her own children. And once again she made her plans. She wanted to learn how to write professionally. It was her dream, and now she wanted to follow it.

So she took courses, and studied and wrote and wrote, prolifically producing and eventually selling her work.

When Jimmy fell ill I sensed a change in Etta. Prayer became like breathing to her, and a prayer chain with friends grew to be a vital part of her life. Faith in God now permeated her own natural strength and courage, and with it, deep peace and utter confidence in God, and because of God, in her own ability.

One more thought. A postscript, if you will, Becky.

Tonight I waltzed with your daddy. It wasn't just any old waltz, either. We swirled and dipped and side-stepped and swayed, lost in the wonder of the music and each other. And then a thought shafted into my mind with amazing clarity. My sister gave me this beautiful moment.

Etta and Jimmy had taught us to waltz.

Later, as your father and I drove home in the darkness of the Texas night, the stars winked down at us, clear and bright as stars can only be in the countryside, away from the city.

Leaning back against the headrest, I closed my eyes and thought again of My Big Sister. Had she also held my hand when I took my first baby steps? I knew beyond a shadow of a doubt that she had helped me get back to my feet in a few dark times as an adult when I felt I couldn't get up again. At those times I heard the echo of her determined voice.

"The Jones kids may get knocked down, but we always, always, get back up again." At those times, I knew I sure wasn't going to let myself be the first Jones kid to stay flat on her face.

How could I face My Big Sister?

On Determination

"I will do this. My Lord will not give me more than I can bear. And when it is over, I will have no regrets.

—*Etta, on caring for her invalid husband*

"Within a few weeks of your Uncle Jimmy's death, Etta determined to live this 'second life' alone to the fullest. The dark curtains Jimmy preferred came down, replaced with shining new ones. The rooms got a new coat of paint and the house took on the brightness and vitality of her personality.

Having set things in order, she seemed to mentally dust off her hands, and she made an announcement. At age 74, to all of us who spent so much time over the years watching her with mouths wide open anyway, she said, 'I'm going to college.'"

—*Ruthie, in a letter to Becky*

*Mom, you're going to give me
gray hair before I'm fourteen.*
—Rachel Praise, my daughter

16

A Sweet Pea in PJs

Sometimes I look at my daughter, Rachel Praise, and wonder when and where this beautiful young woman blossom emerged.

Rachel came into the world with a timing all her own, born so quickly that Scott delivered her himself.

She was a talkative, animated child. To me, that is.

To the rest of the world she might as well have been a deaf-mute, so stubborn and shy was she about speaking in public. She was three-and-a-half years old before she verbalized a single word to her own daddy. Until this point, she and Scott managed to communicate with hugs and grins and much shaking of heads and pointing. He never forced her to talk to him, sure she would speak when she had something she couldn't tell with her eyes. "Besides," he would say as he rocked her in loving silence, "I enjoy the quiet."

The big coming out occurred when Scott read a favorite book to Rachel one evening, and purposely misread the title. Instead of "Vera the Mouse," he read "Vera the Moose." Now the one thing little Rachel could not bear was to let a mistake go by undetected and so, when much head shaking and eye blinking and finger pointing failed to get her daddy to read the title correctly, she blurted out, "It's Vera the mouse, Daddy. Mouse, mouse, mouse, MOUSE!!"

Rachel Praise, age 3, with Scott

What a difference a dozen years makes.

At almost fourteen, Rachel looks like she walked out of the pages of a teen magazine and into our living room. Her long strawberry blond hair flows in gorgeous ringlets, Amy Grant style. She has a frighteningly perfect figure, the kind that looks like it just exited a Barbie Dreamhouse. And *talk*—oh boy, is this girl verbal. If she's not talking to a member of the family, she's hooked up to the telephone IV, the ever present lifeline to her friends.

However, she still greatly prefers things be done decently and in order. Besides wanting words pronounced correctly, Rachel likes her room organized, keeps her school work filed, and has a running list of what she will wear to school every day for the next two weeks (to avoid the disastrous embarrassment of accidentally wearing the same thing twice within a fourteen-day period).

For readers familiar with my work, who know I've basically made a career out of flubbing up, I am what a child like Rachel refers to as a "Challenging Parent." I often exasperate her to the point of near breakdown.

When I forget things—like my name or phone number or what time I was supposed to pick her up at school—I try to console her by saying, "Look Honey, I am out of my mind, but I'll be back in five minutes." To which she replies with a worried look, "Does Alzheimer's run in our genes?" I tell her she might want to start taking gingko biloba just in case—as soon as I can remember to buy some, that is, which might take a few months.

Not long after my trip to Nashville with my sister, I received yet another call asking me if I'd like to come to Tennessee to speak at a sales conference. The publisher said they'd even pay for a companion ticket if I'd be willing to stay over the weekend (thus reducing the total airfare). Scott and I had just enjoyed a recent overnight getaway, so I asked my then thirteen-year-old daughter if she'd like to be my designated companion.

She looked dubious. "Mom, are you sure you can get both of us to the airport and get a rental car and follow a map and all that?"

"Yes, Rachel," I responded, a little hurt by her lack of confidence. "And, this may come as a shock to you, but I can comb my own hair and tie my shoes too."

"It's just that, well, Mother, I don't want you to forget me somewhere in a big city like Nashville. It's okay in Lone Oak; I can always get a ride. But I don't want to be lost in a big city."

"Hey, didn't your Aunt Rachel and I have the time of our lives in Nashville? I've gotten so travel savvy you won't even recognize your ol' Mom. Trust me. You'll be in the hands of a traveling expert."

So we packed our bags and headed out for our first ever mother-daughter out-of-state trip.

What did Rachel want to see in Nashville? Hey, she was almost fourteen.

A night of grinnin' and banjo pickin' at the Grand Ole Opry wasn't exactly her cup of cider.

In this city rich in entertainment and history, it took all of five seconds for Rachel to flip through brochures and make her sightseeing selection. Her choice? The Great American Outlet Mall. We must have spent five hours walking and shopping and trying on clothes. Missed nary a nook, cubby, or cranny. Since I, too, am more bargain hunter than history buff, we were two happy chicks. Had an absolute ball at that mall.

Then the sun went down, the air grew nippy, our stomachs began growling, and our feet began begging for relief. Suddenly, a hot meal and a warm hotel room sounded unbelievably blissful, so we hoisted up our bags and headed to the rental car.

"Do you think the hotel will have a Jacuzzi?" Rachel asked as she struggled to make the last few feet to the car.

"I bet they do, Babe," I replied with good cheer as I fumbled through my purse for my keys. "We'll have to check that out, won't we? Hey, Rachel, you don't have the keys, do you?"

"What?!?"

"I can't seem to find the keys to the car."

"Mom, tell me this is a joke."

Sadly, slowly, I shook my head. A gust of cold wind sent chills up our aching spines as we trudged back toward the mile-long train of stores.

An hour-and-a-half later, after retracing every step we'd taken through every outlet nook, cubby, and cranny, I found the precious keys in the corner of a dressing room.

Exhausted and frozen, our stomachs now screaming for food, we fell into the car with twin sighs of relief.

"Mom?" Rachel asked, her voice trembling from fatigue and cold.

"Yes, Honey."

"You are going to give me gray hair before I'm fourteen."

I smiled weakly and started the engine.

As I drove toward the hotel, the subject of food was foremost on our minds.

"Where would you like to go for dinner, Rachel? I could take you to the Finezza, or how about a little Thai place I love—or would you rather go to a fancy restaurant at Opryland?"

"Do they have any drive-through hamburger places in Nashville?" came my daughter's pitiful, but predictable, response.

So on our first big night away in a city filled with fancy eateries, we drove through a fast-food joint and ordered six greasy Krystal burgers with fries. Then we headed to the hotel to enjoy our feast. But on our way, we decided to make a quick stop at a local five-and-ten for colas, Crayolas, and a couple of coloring books.

Once settled in our room we took turns taking luxurious hot baths and washing our hair. We toweled up our tresses, turban style, then donned warm jammies and robes and snuggly house slippers. I flipped on the television, a special treat for us since we are one of those near-extinct families who do not have TV in their home. (As I related in *A View from the Porch Swing*, a few years back our television was continually struck by lightening—until one day, after the third strike, even as smoke was billowing from the back of the scorched set, it occurred to us this might be a sign from God. Reluctant to pray for a fourth confirmation, we chose not to have it repaired.)

This particular night two consecutive Christmas specials were airing. One was *Touched By an Angel,* the other, a charming based-on-real-events story called *A Thousand Men and a Baby.*

As we settled in to enjoy the programs, we spread our burgers and fries across the nightstand between our two double beds. To this main course, I added some gourmet side dishes, treats I'd purchased at the outlet mall: sesame crackers, jalapeño jelly, and a spicy hummus dip. (My mama used to call me her little Pepper Belly. Indeed, I seem to have been blessed with a fireproof gullet.)

Rachel and I whiled away the evening like two girls at a slumber party. We enjoyed the movies, munched happily on our goodies, and colored pictures to our hearts' content. I distinctly remember thinking, "These are the kind of moments a mother lives for."

I looked up from my coloring book at one point, to see Rachel had been organizing her side of the room. Her clothes were folded and stacked in neat little squares and triangles, like a nice assortment of fabric finger sandwiches. Her makeup and toiletries were arranged on the shelf in perfect ascending and descending order. Even her bedcovers were straight and smooth as she sat crossed-legged on them, smelling of citrus body lotion and fresh shampoo.

"Honey," I smiled, "you—and your side of the room—look like you've been touched by an angel."

Rachel glanced in my direction, raising one eyebrow (a trick she inherited from her feisty Granny). My bed was in crumpled disarray. The suitcase stood open at one corner, spewing clothes on the bedspread. Cracker crumbs and bits of jalepeño jelly stuck to the front of my old nightshirt. I licked a bit of stray hummus from my finger as I asked, "What are you thinking, Sweetheart?"

"I'm thinking," my daughter declared in an even, parental tone, "that it looks like a thousand men and a baby just had a party on your side of the room."

We are the Mother/Daughter Odd Couple, I thought with a smile, kicking the suitcase off the side of the bed to make more room for my feet.

In spite of our differences in personality, Rachel and I had a wonderful time and our weekend drew to a close much too soon. As we stood in line at the Nashville airport to check our luggage and get our boarding passes, recounting our happy memories, a most unpleasant thing occurred. My suitcase exploded.

You see, though my suitcase zipped up quite nicely before I left home, by the time I'd stuffed it with outlet mall loot in

Nashville, Rachel and I had to sit on the edges to get it to close for the return trip. As I approached the ticket counter, the suitcase declared, "I can't take this anymore!" and let go its contents with an audible rip.

If you want to mortify a teenager, try sitting on the floor surrounded by well-groomed businessmen and women, with your lace bras and silk underwear scattered about you. At this point, Rachel excused herself, saying she had to go powder her nose. While she was gone, the ticket lady handed me a large roll of silver duct tape and instructed me to sweep the mess of my wardrobe over to the sidelines until I was able to pull myself together. (I determined not to cry over spilt silk.)

As I struggled to restuff the suitcase, wrapping every inch of it, round and round, with yards of tape, I felt like a life-size caricature in one of Jeff Foxworthy's books. "You know yur a redneck if . . . you latch yur Samsonite with duct tape!" I caught a glimpse of Rachel, several yards off to the side, looking casually about her, occasionally nodding and smiling in my direction as if to say to passersby, "I wonder who that poor imbecile could be?"

Once our luggage had been taped and bedded in the hull of the airplane, my daughter agreed to walk by my side once again. We made the airplane ride home to Dallas without a hitch. We hit the second hitch back at the Dallas-Fort Worth Airport, when I could not remember where I had parked our car.

"No." That was all Rachel could say when I informed her of this fact. "No, no, no, no . . ."

"I'm so sorry," I explained, "but we were in such a hurry when we drove to the airport, and I just kind of forgot to check where we parked. Here, now, don't cry. Chin up! We'll find it."

We spent the next two hours walking up and down endless rows of parked vehicles, pulling and pushing and shoving our backpacks and suitcases (one of them, as you know, looking like something even a cat wouldn't drag in). Finally, we developed a sort of emergency strategy. I would leave Rachel sitting by the pile of suitcases, while I ran back and forth looking for our car. Then we'd haul the baggage down a few more yards and she'd luggage-sit, while I sprinted and searched again.

Upon returning from one of my search and run missions, I found my tired daughter sitting atop the duct-taped luggage, looking like an orphan of some foreign war, soberly munching on what appeared to be a sugar cookie.

"Honey," I asked, "where'd you get that?"

"A lady just walked by," Rachel said, deadpan. "She saw me, then stopped, and said—real sweet—'Honey, you look like you could use a cookie.'" Here Rachel breathed a sigh of exasperation as she put her head in her hands. "Mom, she thought I was homeless."

Just when we thought we would both despair, with no helpful attendants or fresh cookie rations in sight, I caught a glimpse of something familiar. "Rachel!" I shouted. "See that car over there, the one covered with dust?"

"Is it—"

"I think so!"

We both ran toward the car, panting and laughing like two desert refugees who just spied an oasis. I opened the trunk with a flourish, my energy renewed, and together we filled it with our heavy burdens. Once inside the car, I looked over at my daughter and beamed.

"Rachel," I began my heartfelt speech, "I know the last few hours have been difficult. But together, we made it. We bonded in this time of trial, like men in foxholes do during battles. Now that we've survived this, I know you and me, Rachel—we can handle anything life throws at us."

She nodded and gave me a brave little grin. *That's my girl*, I thought.

Then I inserted the keys into the ignition and turned them. Nothing happened.

"Mom?" came the tiny voice from the passenger's seat.

"Mom, please tell me you didn't leave the lights on while we were gone."

"Oops," was all I could manage to say. Drawing on my dwindling reserves of optimism, I said, "Now, let's not give up here, Honey. This isn't the end. We're a traveling team. We're Thelma and Louise, we're Helen Keller and Annie Sullivan, we're—"

"Dumb and Dumber," came the sullen reply.

By the time we got home from Nashville to our home in Greenville, it was three A.M. We could have easily driven home from Nashville in the same amount of time it took us to actually fly, walk, search and run, walk some more, wait for the airport police, get recharged and drive home. Oh, let's be frank: we probably could have *crawled* home and made better time.

But a mere forty-eight hours or so after our return, Rachel actually began speaking to me again.

By the end of her eighth-grade year, Rachel had forgotten most of the indignities she'd suffered at my hand and allowed me to help her prepare for her eighth-grade graduation. In her small school district, eighth-grade graduations are mighty big deals, occasions filled with pomp and circumstance and prom-style party dresses. They are exact replicas of high school graduations, only the girls are much taller than most of the boys.

Lone Oak Middle School's graduation ceremony was held in the gymnasium. I sat at the top of the bleachers, with Scott and our sons and both sets of grandparents to watch our beautiful daughter walk across the stage for her diploma. We'd spent the day finding the perfect dress—gauzy and feminine, lilac flowers on a backdrop of cream—and I'd fixed her auburn curls on top of her head in a Victorian-style upsweep. I brought along a camera just so I could capture this special moment on film, for all time.

"Scott," I whispered, just before our daughter was to rise and go forth for her diploma, "I want to get a close-up of Rachel. I'm going to sneak down to the bottom of the bleachers real quietly and snap a photo."

Just then, a recording of "You'll Never Walk Alone" began playing. (Our school is too small for a genuine choir. We rely on our jam boxes to carry us through these traditional proceedings.) I swallowed a lump in my throat as I stood and began walking down the steps. "When you walk through a storm, hold your head up high . . ."

I thought of all the storms my daughter and I had braved together over the years and couldn't help mouthing the words as I slipped closer toward Rachel, camera in hand. "And don't be afraid of the dark. At the end of the storm is a golden sky and the sweet silver song of a—"

Thump, thump, thump, thump, thump, thump. CLUNK. "OUCH!"

I'd tripped and fallen down about seven steps when I reached the bottom of the bleachers in a final, most undignified thud. My ankle was bleeding, my camera was lying on the ground, every eye was turned in my direction. I gave a brave little wave, reached for my camera, and snapped a picture of my daughter, who was staring into the lens like a deer caught in headlights.

All around me I heard people whispering.

"Was that Rachel's mother?"

"Is she okay?"

"Isn't she the one who writes those funny books?"

"Didn't she fall off the fence at Zeke's football game?"

With as much dignity as I could muster, I ignored the whispers, ascended the steps with the grace of a princess, and took my place back among the family.

"That was touching," Scott murmured. "I'm sure Rachel will always remember it."

"My ankle is bleeding," I countered, hoping to milk some sympathy.

"Poor Peeky," he replied softly, gently putting a hanky over my wound.

I forced myself to look up again. To my great relief and surprise, Rachel was smiling and laughing and shaking her head. She appeared to be taking my public fall in stride.

That evening we hosted a party for the junior high graduates at our home. One by one Rachel and her friends filed by the kitchen and offered condolences for my banged-up ankle and congratulations on a "way cool" party.

After most of the guests had gone home and the kitchen was clean and quiet, I hobbled to Rachel's bedroom door and knocked. I could hear noise, but there was no answer, so I opened the door and walked in. There on the floor sat four chatty, leggy, teenage girls dressed in their PJs, all talking at once and recapping the night in minute detail.

"Did you see Kerri's hair? It was SOOOOOO cute."

"I had my picture taken with Coach Murray."

"Me too!"

Finally, they noticed my presence.

"Hi, Mrs. Freeman!"

"Hi, girls," I replied as I leaned against a poster of some current male heartthrob. "Did you have fun?"

"We had a blast."

"And do you forgive me for humiliating you, Rachel?"

"Mom," Rachel said sweetly, rising to give me a hug. "I don't get embarrassed as much anymore. You made me laugh tonight and everyone thought it was just hilarious. Besides, you landed very gracefully and you got up and back to your seat really fast."

What a relief. I'm moving up from "Embarrassing Mom" to "Slow-witted and Clumsy but Hilarious Mom."

As I bid the girls goodnight, and pulled her door closed behind me, I couldn't help thinking, *My daughter is raising me well.*

On a Mom and Daughter's Best Traveling Tip: Humor

"Enter self-seriousness, exit humor. Exit humor, exit sanity."

—*William Kirk Kilpatrick*

"Laughter is the corrective force which prevents us from becoming cranks."[1]

—*Henri Bergson*

"With the fearful strain that is on me night and day, if I did not laugh I should die."[2]

—*Abraham Lincoln*

Part 4

Georgia Girls'
Reunion

As clearly as God has ever spoken to me,
I knew He was saying, "It is time to create
a home just for you, Seth, and Logan."
—Tina Clark

Logan, Tina, and Seth

17

Forget-Me-Not Stars

*I*t had been a little more than a year since the original "Magnolias" had gathered at Callaway Gardens. It was time for another girls talk-a-thon, this time to catch up on what God had done in our lives since the butterfly prayers.

First stop, Forsyth, Georgia, to see Tina Clark and her boys, Seth and Logan. My sister Rachel had flown in the night before I drove down from a ladies conference I had keynoted in Atlanta. (Feeling quite proud of my travel-savvy self, I might add. I only lost my keys one time.)

There's something about this part of Georgia that slows one's pace, makes one pause and breathe in great gulps of fresh air. It's a place that invites folks to collapse on porch swings 'til the crickets and frogs and owls come out to sing and croak and hoot, serenading the evening away.

Tina's country home backed up to woods alive with orange, red, and yellow colors this crisp October weekend. Her flower and herb garden lined the fence invitingly. Seth walked over to greet me, arm outstretched like a country gentleman, to shake hands in greeting. He was thirteen, dark eyes, thick eyebrows, movie star handsome. James Dean kind of appeal. At ten, Logan was handsome like his brother, and especially wired. He was so excited to have company (even if "company" was two middle-aged sisters), and as friendly as the three puppy dogs that bounded out to greet me with licks and yelps for ear rubs.

Tina had chili simmering on the kitchen stove and a fire in the hearth. Her home was every Southern woman's dream. A large country kitchen with deep green-and-white checked floors overlooked a sitting room, where I found Rachel cozied up with a book. I paused to reach out and give my sister a hug. "How are you and my sweet brother-in-law?"

She returned my steady gaze, her eyes sparkling. "After taking a hard look at ourselves and making some major changes—we are doing great."

"Good!" I teased. "I'm calling YOU for advice the next time Scott and I hit an impasse."

As I continued on Tina's "Better Homes" tour (her home sure looked better than mine anyway), a long comfy-looking window seat caught my eye. I had wished for such a perfect nook when I was a girl of nine or ten, a place to pore over books like *Little Women* or sit and look longingly out the window. A perfect backdrop for dramatic sulking.

The living room was Norman Rockwell homey. An enormous couch of deep green-and-ivory-checked fabric sat in front of the fireplace, sandwiched between old-timey rocking chairs. Big chunky candles of burgundy and cream were lit, casting a warm golden glow on the wooden dining table in another corner.

"Tina, this place is incredible!" I said, punctuating every sentence with an *ooh* or a *wow*. As she showed me her bedroom, painted sunny yellow, and her connecting bathroom, done up in Wedgwood blue and white, she said, "This was our therapy, building this home. A year after Wyndell died I was driving home and it just hit me, 'Sell the house and build a new home. Make a new life for you and the boys.'"

"I think you're so brave," I said sincerely. "You must have felt like a pioneer woman, homesteading new ground with the help of your sons."

Tina smiled and nodded, explaining, "Our old house held our original family: Wyndell and me and the boys. But months after the funeral, at six in the evening, I found my eyes automatically turning to the front door, my subconscious expecting Wyndell home from work. I needed to get away from that front door and the bittersweet memories that seeped out of every wall. As clearly as God has ever spoken to me, I knew He was saying, 'It is time to create a home just for you, Seth, and Logan.'

"Wyndell's life was so precious—being his wife for ten years helped me become who I am now. So I want my life and the way we live it—the boys' lives too—to be a tribute to him. He didn't get a chance to go on to live and be thirty-five and forty and see his grandkids, but we have an opportunity to live our lives well as a tribute to his memory."

Seth and Logan came bounding in just then, asking me if I'd like to see their woods. I quickly agreed and within minutes found myself surrounded by tall trees and crunchy leaves, a wooded dreamland.

"Here's our rope swing." Seth pointed to a rope dangling from a branch high above our heads.

"Yeah," said Logan, "your sister Rachel swung on it a while ago." He said it as a dare, and I did not hesitate to take him up on the offer, grabbing up the swing and putting my foot in the loop of the rope, hoping I didn't break a leg just to keep pace with my little sister.

It was a "wheeee!" kind of moment, a brief interlude of childlike abandon.

Soon after our hike, Seth took off for a church party leaving Tina and Rachel and me chaperoned by little Logan, who was having a royal fit for us to "go outside and see the stars!"

"Logan," Tina kept saying, "it's not dark enough yet. Wait a little longer . . ."

"But Mama," he'd echo, "we might miss 'em!"

All through dinner and a little while into dessert (brown and orange M&Ms from a bag, with fresh hot coffee), Logan kept up the consistent begging for us to "go out and see the stars."

"What is it with him and stars?" I finally asked Tina.

Reaching toward the bookshelf, Tina pulled out a slim volume.

"Before Wyndell died he read a passage from this book, *The Little Prince,* and loved it so much, he asked that we read it at his funeral, to comfort me and the boys. I gave Seth and Logan each a copy the day their daddy died."

Tina found the passage and read aloud, her Southern accent adding to the timeless charm of the words.

"All men have stars," he answered, "but they are not the same things for different people . . . You—you alone—will have the stars as no one else has them . . .

"In one of the stars I shall be living. In one of them I shall be laughing. And so it will be as if all the stars were laughing, when you look at the sky at night . . . You—only you—will have stars that can laugh!

"And when your sorrow is comforted (time soothes all sorrows) you will be content that you have known me. . . You will want to laugh with me. And you will sometimes open your window . . . And your friends will be properly astonished to see you laughing as you look up at the sky!"[1]

Tina put the book down and glanced out the window, declaring it was now dark enough. She grabbed up a quilt and we all followed her out the door, a parade of three women, one boy, three dogs, and three cats. We spread the quilt on the front lawn and each found a spot to lie down as various pets snuggled up near us, creating lumps of warm fur to pillow our heads. It was a cold night and exceptionally clear. Stars scattered like hundreds of tiny lighthouses across a sea of black.

By the light of the moon, I watched in amazement as Logan relaxed under the sky's lovely spell. He reminded me of a hungry baby pacified by a bottle of warm milk—limbs all limp and thankful. If his ten-year-old body could speak, every cell would be saying, "Ahhhhhhhhhhhhhhhhhh . . . now *that's* more like it."

"Have you always loved stars?" I asked to anyone and everyone, my eyes searching the sky for the Big and Little Dippers.

"Yep," Tina said. "I've always been a sky person. Clouds float my boat too."

"Me too," I heard Logan mumble quietly near the ear of his pudgy little dachshund. "I'm a sky person too."

Just like your Daddy, I thought. *Oh, Lord, let there be windows in heaven tonight. May Wyndell catch a glimpse of his family, happily looking above—and may they, too, catch glimpses of their daddy and husband, shining brightly above all the stars.*

Later, as we sat around the fireplace after our time under the stars, I remembered Tina's prayer request from our time in Callaway—that she would continue to feel God's nearness and move through the grief process to a time of complete healing. I asked her how that was coming.

"Really well," Tina said, pulling an afghan around her legs. "I had all this love I'd showered on Wyndell, and it needed a place to go. God's been so good to give me outlets for that love."

As she spoke, I learned that Tina was not only star gazing those days, she was teaching classes on grief recovery, and flourishing in her work as a teacher of emotionally disturbed children. "Those kids and I understand each other," Tina said with a wink. She planned to host a house full of boys to eat pizza and watch wrestling matches later that weekend. If not perfect, life was very, very good.

Now comfortable enough to ask Tina anything, I wanted to know how a widow copes without romantic love, only we decided to use a code word because Logan's young ears were near.

"How about we call sex, 'cholesterol'?" she whispered.

"Gotcha," I said softly, then asked aloud, "So how does it feel to live cholesterol-free?"

Tina giggled and said, "It's amazing, really. I mean I used to

LOVE cholesterol. Had it regularly. Though never quite enough for Wyndell. He used to tease me by saying, 'Babe, it's going to be my luck that you'll reach your, uh, cholesterol peak while I'm off on a trip and I'll miss it.' Well, there were a couple of years when I really did miss cholesterol, but I've adjusted really well. Don't even think about cholesterol all that much anymore. It's amazing really. The Lord seems to have adjusted my cholesterol cravings to fit my new life."

At this point both of us were laughing and holding on to the couch cushions for support. Logan just looked up with a curious grin.

Later, after he is asleep, Tina shares that the most difficult part of widowhood, at this stage, is the boys' need for a father figure. "Thankfully, a big-hearted dad in my church, Cole, has formed a bond with Logan. Seth is very close to my father, and I'm so thankful for that, but he also needs a guy friend closer to my age to take him to do 'dad stuff' with him. This is the only thing that breaks my heart. The church is full of daddies—and I know they are busy with their own families, but if they only knew how much it means to a fatherless kid to have a man in his life to check in on him, see how he's doing, take him for ice cream or camping or fishing. I thank God every day for Cole."

I could not help thinking of the verse in the first chapter of James. "Pure and undefiled religion before God and the Father is this: to visit orphans and widows in their trouble . . ." (v. 27).

Now that I knew and loved a widow and her children, up close and personal, and watched them searching the sky for memories of their husband and father, those words broke my heart, and gave me new passion to reach out, to encourage men to think about taking one extra child under their arms, and into their hearts.

Surely, more of us can reach out and watch God multiply the love in our lives.

To Grow Up On . . .

Tina wrote a note in the front of Seth and Logan's copy of *The Little Prince*. Her words were so tender and so revealing of Tina's compassionate heart, I asked if I might share them in this book. Tina and the boys graciously agreed. I retype them now as my own eyes fill and overflow with tears.

My Dear Sons,
I am so sorry that the first hurt in your life had to be such a terribly deep one.

Just always know how very much your daddy loved you. He was so VERY proud of you and had such beautiful dreams for you. You taught your daddy the true meaning of completely selfless love.

Whenever you really miss your daddy, just look up at the stars and he'll be there for you. Always!

Your daddy asked to have the passage from *The Little Prince* read at his funeral. I hope you will always hold these words dear to your heart. "You— you alone will have the stars as no one else has them . . ."

I love you with all my soul,
Mama

Here we were, the week before this book about Southern women friends was due, stepping through the screen doors of the Whistle Stop Café, the old backdrop for the movie Fried Green Tomatoes.
—Becky Freeman

From L to R: Susan, Tina, Seth, Logan, Rachel

18

Refried Magnolias

*T*he next morning, I spoke to Tina's Sunday school class and then we went straight back to her home.

Everyone found a quilt and a bed and a cozy corner and napped until one o'clock. Talking until way past midnight had exhausted us all. Not only that, but Tina's Swiss cuckoo clock—clucking at regular intervals—had nearly catapulted my sanity over the cuckoo's nest the night before. About three or four in the morning, I'd had it with that pesky bird and cheerful wood chopper. I walked to the kitchen, took the clock—with all its five-foot-long swinging pendulums—and locked it in the laundry room.

I slept maybe three hours before dawn.

Have you ever had a nap so perfect you wish it would never end? I lay on a quilted bedspread, the sun pouring in just so, warming the room with a lazy shimmer. Then a big gray cat jumped up on the bed, lazily sprawling over my feet and another, a calico, curled up near the small of my back. The cats' soft purring, the sun shining, and my body aching for rest—it made for an exquisite gourmet napping experience.

Once we had our rest, Tina, Rachel, the boys, and I—the whole lot of us—drove out to a tiny town near a railroad station in Juliette, Georgia, to eat lunch at none other than the Whistle

Stop Café. Just before we were seated, a familiar lady with a Calgon face walked up on the café's porch.

"Susan!" we all yelled at once, hugging her close as we entered the café.

I could hardly believe it.

Here I was, the week before this book about Southern women friends was due to land on my editor's desk, stepping through the screen doors of the Whistle Stop Café, the old backdrop for the movie *Fried Green Tomatoes*.

An old-fashioned diner counter with bar stools was in the center of the café, with booths scattered around the perimeter. As we sat near a window overlooking the small row of quaint shops—including one named "The Magnolias"—I saw a light blue Studebaker pull up to the curb, completing the feeling of having stepped into the 1930s.

"Susan," I said, as we looked through the menu and caught up on our lives, "tell me about your butterfly prayer. How's Doug's job situation?"

"Becky," she answered, a grateful expression crossing her face. "He got a new job about eight months ago and he absolutely loves it."

"Well," I replied, "I have an answer to prayer to report too. Though my writing and speaking is still wild with activity, God has been teaching me the art of resting on the run. Showing me that productivity and ministry flow best when my mind is centered. Also, I committed this year to take summers and the month of December off to just be with my kids."

"We could start a butterfly magnet phenomena, you know it?" Tina said.

"Send us your butterflies," Rachel mimicked the voice of a TV evangelist, "and we let the Georgia Girls put hands on them and pray for your needs!"

"Listen," Susan laughed, "all I know is, I'm calling you guys the next time I need prayer."

The waitress came out bearing mason jars of sweet tea over crushed ice with a lemon perched jauntily on the edge of the glass. After the appetizer of fried green tomatoes (fast becoming my favorite vegetable), came barbequed chicken, turnip greens, baked beans, corn bread, and peach cobbler—topped off with a steaming mug of hot coffee. If I'd been a man, and not a lady of genteel Southern breeding, I might have belched from pure satisfaction.

The day, too, was perfection—just the way I like the air—cool and warm at the same time. Invigorating. I could live outside all day in this kind of weather.

After lunch we moved to the porch to take pictures and make evening plans.

"Listen," Susan said, "Maureen and Suzanne want you all to come over for supper tonight in Barnesville. We'll have sandwiches and you can see our husbands and kids. And Maureen has a surprise for you too."

"Sounds great," I nodded, then looked at my sister and Tina. "What do y'all think?"

Rachel agreed it was a good idea, and we decided she and I would spend the night at Suzanne's who lived a few doors down from Maureen. Tina had to decline; she was expecting a house full of teenagers to watch the wrestling match. It dawned on me how hard it is to be the one and only parent. There's never a time when Tina can say, "Sure I'll come, my husband can watch the boys." Again I prayed for more sensitivity to single mothers. How easy to forget the burden they carry, how I take my own husband so often for granted.

As Rachel and I drove up the road to Barnesville, I wondered about Maureen's butterfly prayer. All around her, her friends were adopting children. Tina revealed, over lunch, that she and the boys were hoping to become a foster family. Three out of the four Magnolias were fostering or adopting children. What were the chances that Maureen would make it an even four?

"I heard Bobby and Maureen have befriended a precious little eight-year-old boy named Phillip in Garth and Suzanne's church," I said to my sister, musing aloud as I drove.

"Really?" she asked.

"Yes, his only living relative is an aging grandmother. Bobby is so good with kids—did you know he was the coach of the winningest college basketball team in Georgia? Anyway, they fell in love with Phillip and are now 'Aunt Maureen and Uncle Bobby' to him. The grandmother has appointed Bobby and Maureen to be Phillip's legal guardians upon her death."

"Do you think that will be enough for Maureen?" Rachel asked aloud what I was already thinking. "I mean do you think being close to Phillip will satisfy that longing to be a full-time mother right now?"

"It will help," I answered. "But no, I don't think it will be enough."

I drove up to the gingerbread cottage whose porch was gaily decorated with pumpkins and Indian corn. This Magnolia could beautify everything she touched. Rachel and I walked up the porch steps and before we could knock, the front door opened and there stood Maureen.

Holding a remarkably beautiful baby girl in her arms.

The baby, with skin of peaches and cream, had wisps of dark hair, deep blue eyes, and a perfect rosebud mouth. Dressed in soft pale pink, she was quite the picture.

Rachel and I stopped and stared, our mouths agape. "Maureen?" I asked. "Is she yours?" Rachel followed up.

Maureen nodded her head up and down, slowly, her smile lighting up her face, tears beading at the corner of her big blue eyes. "Is she not a blessin'? Seven months old and the best baby you ever saw."

Within minutes I was in a rocking chair, holding Allie Re, feeding her a bottle as she reached her chubby hands for my earrings, swallowing me with her blue eyes, like pools of deep water.

"Becky," Maureen said, as she leaned against her husband

Bobby on the living room sofa, "remember how we prayed for a miracle baby? Actually, I've been praying I would have a baby girl someday since I was thirteen years old. I'm forty now. So Allie's the answer to a twenty-seven-year-old prayer."

"So how did this happen?" I asked, as I fingered Allie's tiny hands.

"It's a long story," began Maureen, "but in a nutshell, after Callaway, Bobby and I decided to go through foster parenting classes. I remember sitting across the desk from Miss Martha, the social worker who helped Susan. Though we were willing to foster parent any child in the system, I was honest with her. 'Miss Martha,' I said. 'I want to adopt a baby girl.'"

"She looked at me, her eyes full of pity and said, 'Maureen, a social worker only gets a couple of miracles in her career. Finding Gregory for Doug and Susan was one of them. The chances that I can find you a baby—especially a Caucasian baby—are zero.'"

"What did you say to that?"

Bobby spoke up. "I'll tell you what she said, Becky. We got in the car and I said to her, 'Honey, now listen, Miss Martha is trying to tell you to be realistic.' And Maureen said to me, 'Bobby, Miss Martha let a tiny bit of air out of my balloon back there, but not much.'"

Maureen was itching to finish the story. "Needless to say, when Miss Martha found Allie Re for us, she called and said, 'I've just had my second miracle in twenty-four years.' Allie will be officially, legally ours in two more weeks. Around Thanksgiving. Is that not perfect? Talk about countin' our blessin's!"

What words are there to express how it feels to be rocking a rosy-cheeked, blue-eyed miracle? As a writer, I find myself frustrated at points like these: how can I describe the feel of a small human being, so soft and vulnerable, wriggling aliveness in your arms?

There was a knock at the door, and another tall handsome

fellow walked in with a miniature version of himself at his side. It was Doug, Susan's husband, with little three-year-old Gregory. Gregory toddled up to me, as I held out my arms, and smiled shyly. I reached out to stroke his soft brown hair. What a child. What a gorgeous child. He wore the tiniest pair of blue jeans and as he stood in front of me, he smiled, reached deep into his pocket, and pulled out a small baggie of pennies.

"See?" he said.

I saw. I saw another Godsend. I saw a father and mother beaming toward this little boy of their hopes and dreams and prayers.

"Tell Miss Becky what we just did," Doug, the proud father, prompted.

Gregory looked up and grinned, pointing to the sky. "We frooo! We froo in Daddy's airpwane!"

"That's right," Doug interpreted, "We flew in the airplane. He loves to fly—"

"—and it shows." I couldn't help singsonging, with a little airline humor.

The evening was alive with mothers and fathers adoring the children they had prayed into each other's lives. I looked over at Suzanne, who had just entered the room with a plate of chocolate chip cookies. Her hair was layered and brushed up in an attractive style, and she wore a snazzy outfit of deep aqua. She laughed and joked and seemed more at ease than I'd ever seen her before.

"Beck," Rachel whispered as we passed each other on the way to the cookies.

"Yeah?" I asked.

"I think Suzanne has found herself. She looks GREAT."

I laughed and had to agree.

As we chatted over sandwiches, I gave the Barnesville Magnolias their new nickname: "I now officially christen you— The Barnesville Adoptettes."

Then I asked them what they would like to tell other women who long for a child.

"Pray," they all said at once. "Gather a circle of understanding friends and pray for each other."

"If the Lord shows you a child in need of adoption, and tells you deep in your heart, 'This is your child,' don't let anything stop your efforts to bring him into your home. If God is behind it, miracles will happen."

"It may take time, but we are convinced angels work double-time on a child's behalf as we pray and trust and obey God's prompting."

"And don't be afraid."

"Yes, don't be afraid. So many wonderful children go unadopted because of the few horror stories that get media exposure. Sure, some children take extra time and care to adjust and stabilize into a home. But it *can* be done, and *is* being done all the time."

How could I argue with the results? The smiles all over Maureen's living room told the story without words.

The next morning, I awoke in Garth and Suzanne's home to a little girl's voice with a Southern accent as sweet and thick as creamed honey.

"Mornin,' Miss Becky." Savannah said as she reached to give me a hug. "Mornin,' Miss Savannah," I said smiling groggily. "If you don't look pretty this morning!"

"Thank you, ma'am," she said brightly. (The words *sir* and *ma'am* are very much alive in the small towns of Georgia.)

At seven years old, Savannah is truly a remarkable child. She'd read the entire Laura Ingalls Wilder series and *Charlotte's Web* this past summer. She couldn't wait to show me her "novel";

she was working very hard on it, trying to write a chapter a night. It was a delightful story about a pig who lives in the wilderness with a little girl named Laura—sort of a *Wilbur Goes to Little House on the Prairie* concept. (We writers do tend to draw inspiration from what we are reading at the time.)

With generous doses of love and discipline, Garth and Suzanne were raising their little girl with sweetness, charm, and an imagination to rival Shirley Temple.

Savannah also entertained me—and herself—as we enjoyed our morning visit, with a family of imaginary dolphins swimming around the twin bed we were sitting on. (As I met each member of the invisible dolphin family, she asked me to please be careful not to accidentally sit on a fin. Only in Savannah-speak, it came out more like "Miss Becky, would you ple-eese be cayerful nah-ut to see-ut on a feeeeun?")

Soon, Brent came in to join the party. His blond hair gave his chiseled face, complete with dimples, an irresistible Beach Boy look. Though modest, I could tell when I asked him point-blank, he was not hurting for female admirers in his high school.

Brent is, in fact, the kind of kid you want to wrap your arms around and take home with you. (Which, in retrospect, is what the Forsters did.) He's funny and kind and polite—loves the Lord, his family and friends, his golden retriever (Honey), his computer, card tricks, his classic red Buick, and girls. (Though not necessarily in that order.)

As I sat in this little girl's bedroom—all pink roses and lace and froufrou—visiting and laughing with two happy kids, I thought, *What a neat way to wake up. Even better than a cup of strong coffee with cream.*

Later that day, after saying good-byes to the Georgia Girls and their gents and kids, Rachel and I headed toward the airport. I would drive us to Atlanta, drop Rachel off for her flight to Virginia, then turn in the rental car and catch my plane home to Texas.

"So, Beck, how will you end the book?" Rachel asked.

"I don't know," I replied thoughtfully. The weekend had been so full, I felt as though I had been handed a mile-deep glacier and could only reveal two feet of it. The hardest work of writing is not deciding what to tell; it is the agony of choosing what must be left out.

"Rachel," I asked aloud as I navigated the freeway, "help me brainstorm here."

"Okay," my sister said, always knowing exactly how to prime the pump of my thoughts. "What's the green vine connecting all these Magnolias, these women whose stories you share?"

I began to talk freely, thinking aloud.

"Rachel, this is a book about the power of friendships between women. It is about the incredible gifts we give each other.

"It's how childless women pray for one another until every last one of them is mothering a son or daughter.

"It's about women of courage, who in the midst of great grief, continue to reach toward life.

"It is about a mother so compassionate she sacrifices her kidney to help her neighbor's child live and laugh and hug her parents and play softball.

"It is about my close circle of friends who help me to lighten up with laughter and hold me, pray for me, let me cry freely—with a minimum of advice—when I am feeling overwhelmed.

"It is about women I admire from afar—role models of encouragement echoing, 'You can do this Becky!' as I, a scared little mom from the country, rise to the platform to speak to hundreds of people.

"It's about women who remind me how big God's love is, that I am the apple of my Father's eye. (Who tell me that life really begins at eighty—and paint a future so bright, I want to buy stock in shades.)

"It's about the women in my family, the faith that was bred in my bones, the gifts of laughter and storytelling and courage to change and grow that I inherited from Nonnie, Aunt Etta,

Mother—and share back and forth with you. These gifts I hope to pass on to my daughter Rachel.

"In short, it is about the impact we have on one another, women to women. And my desire to value that more and more. To foster other circles of friendships across the country—or perhaps to encourage young women to start their own circle of Magnolia friends.

"Then I'd write that," Rachel said, with an emphatic declaration.

"You know what," I said, smiling at her just before I drove up to the baggage check area. "I think I will."

And, as you can see—

I did.

Maureen and Allie Ré

On Real Friendship

Anyone can stand by you when you are right, but a friend will stand by you even when you are wrong . . .

A simple friend identifies himself when he calls.
    A real friend doesn't have to.

A simple friend thinks the problems you whine about are recent.
    A real friend says, "You've been whining about the same thing for years. Get off your duff and do something about it."

A simple friend doesn't know your parents' first names.
    A real friend has their phone numbers in his address book.

A simple friend, when visiting, acts like a guest.
    A real friend opens your refrigerator and helps himself.

A simple friend has never seen you cry.
    A real friend has shoulders soggy from your tears.

A simple friend hates it when you call after he has gone to bed.
    A real friend asks you why you took so long to call.

—(From an e-mail, no source given)

Notes

Chapter 1

1. Arthur Gordon, *A Touch of Wonder,* "Watch Out for Charm" (Old Tappan, NJ: Fleming H. Revell, 1974), 37, 42.

Chapter 2

1. Daniel W. Whittle, 1840–1901, "There Shall Be Showers of Blessing," *The Baptist Hymnal* (Nashville: Convention Press, 1991).

2. Ken Gire, *Reflections on the Word* (Colorado Springs: Chariot Victor Publishing, 1998).

3. Albert Einstein as quoted in *All Things Are Possible,* Barbara Milo Ohrbach (New York: Clarkson N. Potter, 1995), 18.

Chapter 3

1. Since 1974, Big Oak Ranch, located in Gadsden, Alabama, has been home for more than 1,300 children who have been abused, neglected, or abandoned. Big Oak Ranch offers children from ages six to twenty-one a refuge from harm, a break from the hurt, and a natural nurturing environment

for healing. The founder, John Croyle, is a graduate of the University of Alabama, where he was a second team All-American football star. In 1974, he faced one of the most important decisions of his life: whether to play professional football or to start a children's home. John followed the Lord's leadership and gave his life to helping kids. His story has been featured in *Reader's Digest, Sports Illustrated, People,* and *Focus on the Family* magazine. He has also made guest appearances on *The Today Show, CNN News,* ABC Sports' *Half-Time Report,* Robert Schuller's *Hour of Power,* and *The 700 Club.* Big Oak Ranch is operated by gifts from friends, and help from volunteers willing to work alongside staff and resident houseparents.

For more information see *Bring Out the Winner in Your Child,* by John Croyle with Ken Abraham (Nashville: Cumberland House Publishing, Inc., 1996).

Interested in being a houseparent? Sending cards or letters to children? Helping financially? Starting a ranch ministry in your state? Write Big Oak Ranch at 250 Jake Mintz Road, Gadsden, AL 35905-8958 to find out how you can help.

Chapter 4

1. Edward F. Murphy, *2,715 One-Line Quotations for Speakers, Writers and Raconteurs* (New York: Gramercy Books, 1996).

2. *Ibid.*

3. "Reverence for Life," Albert Schweitzer as quoted in *Reflections on the Word,* Ken Gire (Colorado Springs: Chariot Victor Publishing, 1998).

Chapter 5

1. Daniel W. Whittle, 1840-1901, "There Shall Be Showers of

Blessing," *The Baptist Hymnal* (Nashville: Convention Press, 1991).

2. Robert I. Fitzhenry, ed., *The Harper Book of Quotations* (New York: HarperCollins, 1993).

3. *Words of Love II* (New York: Perigree Books, 1994).

4. Alda Ellis, *Always Friends* (Eugene, OR: Harvest House Publishers, 1997).

5. *Ibid.*

Chapter 6

1. This article was adapted from stories written by Gracie Malone and published in *Moody* magazine ("Under Job's Skin") and a chapter ("When My Wings Were Clipped") from the book *Courage for the Chicken-Hearted* by Gracie and me and three of our local "Hens with Pens" friends: Susan Duke, Rebecca Jordan, and Fran Sandin. This book and its sequel were published by Honor Books. (We may be crazy in Greenville, Texas, but we sure do have a good time.)

2. Peter McWilliams, *Life 101* (Los Angeles: Prelude Press, 1996).

3. *Ibid.*

4. *Ibid.*

5. *Ibid.*

Chapter 8

1. Henri Nouwen, *The Wounded Healer: Ministry in Contemporary Society* (Image Books, 1979).

2. Excerpts from *The Velveteen Woman*, by Brenda Waggoner, used by permission of Chariot Victor Publishing, 1999.

3. Brennan Manning, *The Ragamuffin Gospel* (Sisters, OR: Multnomah Books, 1990), 51.

4. Thomas Merton as quoted in *The Ragamuffin Gospel* (Sisters, OR: Multnomah Books, 1990).

Chapter 9

1. I highly recommend "experiencing Suzie" for yourself. For information about her speaking or to order her hilarious, encouraging tapes, contact Catherine Cargile, 817-469-7323, fax 817-795-5113, or write P.O. Box 121502, Arlington, TX 76012.

Chapter 10

1. Used by permission of the National Kidney Foundation Resources. For more information, contact the National Kidney Foundation at 888-829-1299 or the American Kidney Association at 800-822-4685.

Chapter 11

1. Anabel Gillham, *The Confident Woman* (Copyright © 1993 by Anabel Gillham; published by Harvet House Publishers, Eugene, OR 97402). Used by permission. For information on tapes and books by Bill and Anabel Gillham, call 1-888-395-LIFE. Tell 'em Becky sent you, and be sure to give them my love.

2. Henri Nouwen, *In the Name of Jesus* (New York: Crossroad Publishers, 1994).

3. Charles Morgan, *The Harper Book of Quotations*, Robert I. Fitzhenry, ed. (New York: HarperCollins, 1993).

4. Arthur Gordon, *A Touch of Wonder,* "Watch Out for Charm" (Old Tappan, NJ: Fleming H. Revell, 1974).

5. Dr. Bernie Siegal, *The Harper Book of Quotations*, Robert I. Fitzhenry, ed. (New York: HarperCollins, 1993).

6. Jean Anouilh, *The Harper Book of Quotations*, Robert I. Fitzhenry, ed. (New York: HarperCollins, 1993).

Chapter 13

1. Horatio G. Spafford, 1828–1888, "It Is Well with My Soul," *The Baptist Hymnal* (Nashville, TN: Convention Press, 1991).

2. An orphanage for the abandoned AIDS street children of Africa is being built and maintained with funds given to the memory of Bob and Bernie's grandson, Robin and Maxine's son, and Tara's big brother. It is called The House of Joel. For more information:

   Teen Missions
   885 E Hall Rd.
   Merritt Island, FL 32953-8443
   407-453-0350
   Email: tmi@cape.net

3. Vittorio Alfieri source unknown.

4. Catherine Marshall, *To Live Again* (New York: McGraw-Hill, 1957).

5. George Matheson, 1842–1906, "O Love That Wilt Not Let Me Go," *The Baptist Hymnal* (Nashville: Convention Press, 1991).

Chapter 14

1. Sermons and Prayers by Peter Marshall and Catherine Marshall, *Mr. Jones, Meet the Master* (Old Tappan, NJ: Fleming H. Revell, 1949).

Chapter 15

1. Etta Lynch, *Help is Only a Prayer Away*, first printing 1972, reprinted 1998. To order this book or to obtain Etta Lynch's speaking schedule, e-mail elynch@juno.com or write: 5101 E. 41st, Lubbock, TX 79414.

Chapter 16

1. Murphy, *2,715 One-Line Quotations for Speakers, Writers and Raconteurs*.

2. *Ibid.*

Chapter 17

1. Antoine de Saint-Exupery, *The Little Prince* (San Diego: HarBrace, 1943).

About the Author

Becky Freeman, a Texas girl born and bred, speaks fluent Southern. Her popularity as an author, speaker, and media guest comes from her Texas-style storytelling, served up with plenty of ham and a dollop of honey. She writes a column for *Home Life* magazine, has been a regular feature on "Home Life Television," and is the author of seven books, including *Worms in My Tea and Other Mixed Blessings, Still Lickin' the Spoon, Marriage 9-1-1,* and *A View from the Porch Swing.*

She and her husband, Scott, and their four children live in the country near Greenville, Texas.

For information about booking Becky to speak, contact:
Speak Up Speaker Services (Carol Kent, President)
1614 Edison Shores Place
Port Huron, Michigan 48060-3374
Phone: 810-982-0898
E-mail: speakupinc@aol.com

To contact Becky about this book or to send in your own "Real Magnolia" story, send your e-mail to beckyworms@compuserve.com.